THE SILENCE OF THE SUFI

The Silence of the Sufi

by Sabit Madaliev

VOLUME ONE

And I Do Call to Witness the Self-Reproaching Spirit

translated by Russell Scott Valentino

*Æ*B
Autumn Hill Books
Iowa City, Iowa

*Æ*B

http://www.autumnhillbooks.com
Autumn Hill Books, Iowa City, IA 52240
© 2006 by Autumn Hill Books
All Rights Reserved. Published 2006
Printed in the United States of America

Original Title: *Molchanie Sufi* © 2005 by Sabit Madaliev

Library of Congress Control Number 2006932340

Autumn Hill Books ISBN-13: 9780975444429
Autumn Hill Books ISBN-10: 0975444425

Table Of Contents

There are no paths to God for those who have not mastered the rules of politeness and good breeding.

Sufi Tradition

Prelude

In the name of Allah the Compassionate, the Merciful!

The aim of God's creation, so say the wise, was the human being, for only in him could divine beauty be embodied on earth. And for this reason he must strive toward God. Herein lies his destiny, the meaning of his life. And only in striving for God, in unabatedly improving his moral state, moving from betterment to perfection, can the human being become complete, a concentration of all that is bright and holy, the divine on earth.

The perfected human being, our predecessors were convinced, is the best, highest, and noblest of all the Creator's works. At the moment of creation—said Abdurrahman Jami[1] to his followers, may mercy be upon him—God placed in the human soul a tiny bit of each of His own limitless qualities, so that, by that little bit, he, the human being, might understand the great and the infinite, just as one knows all the granary's wheat by a handful of grain and, by a single pitcher full, an entire river's water.

God granted hearing and sight to the human being so that he might correlate the beauty of the earth with the beauty of his soul. And God gave him a heart, by perfecting which and rendering righteous, he might draw near to God and know Truth.

---

1   Jami (d. 1492): Persian mystic, scholar, and poet.

Glory to the messenger of Allah, chosen by the Most High Himself, to lead people to the righteous path. May divine mercy be upon all the *shaikhs*[2] and Sufis of the Naqshbandi Order, who illuminate the righteous path with the light of their pure hearts.

It is said in the *hadith*[3]: According to the testimonial of an-Havvas ibn Saman,[4] may mercy be upon him, the Prophet, may Allah bless him and send him peace, said:

Righteousness is proper moral foundation, while transgression is that which stirs in your soul and which you do not want others to know of.[5]

The following *hadith* is quoted in the *musnads*[6] of the two imams Ahmad ibn Hanbal and ad-Damiri.[7] According to the testimonial of Wabisa bin Mabad,[8] may mercy

2   *Shaikh*: Sufi mentor and teacher.
3   *Hadith* (pl. *ahadith*): compiled record of the sayings and deeds of the Prophet Muhammad, revered as a major source of moral guidance and religious law.
4   An-Havvas ibn Saman (also 'Abd Allah ibn al'Abbas, d. ca. 687): Companion of the Prophet Muhammad.
5   Cited in the *Sahih* of Muslim ibn al-Hajjaj (d. 875).
6   *Musnad*: early compilation of *ahadith*, categorized not by subject but by the Companion of Muhammad to whom they were attributed.
7   Ahmad ibn Hanbal (d. 855) and Muhammad ibn Musa Kamal Ad-din ad-Damiri (d. 1405).
8   Wabisa bin Mabad: Companion of the Prophet Muhammad.

be upon him, who said, "I came to the Messenger of Allah, may Allah bless him and send him peace, and he said, 'You've come to ask about righteousness?'

"'Yes,' I answered.

"He said, 'Ask your heart! Righteousness is what the soul is not troubled by and the heart is not troubled by, while transgression is what stirs in the soul, what tosses and turns in your chest, even after people have told you many times that, in their opinion, you have acted lawfully.'"

✦ ✦ ✦

With trepidation in my heart I appeal to the deeds and words, the blessed mystery of our holy predecessors' mystical states, from our Shaikh Ibrahim even unto the Prophet Muhammad, may Allah bless and greet him. My modest knowledge is limited to oral and written accounts, to conversations in the *hanaqa*,[9] to my own modest investigations, and to the golden grains of wisdom that overflow from the pages of those folios that have been preserved.

My appeal to the memory of our teachers derives as well from the wish that our children should know more about them than about their fathers. The destiny of an earthly father is the development and continuation of humanity. But the *shaikh* is a spiritual father who develops the divine principle in a person and directs him on the path of the righteous.

9 *Hanaqa*: Sufi lodge.

Sufis are convinced that religious ties among people are more durable than ties of kinship and blood. The spiritual kinship between us, the people of today, and our glorious predecessors, the great Sufis, will not be realized or constituted—Sufis say—until we do as they did, until we at least attempt to follow the path that they followed, and according to their teachings. But in order to follow their righteous path, one must assimilate the moral qualities of these noble ones, thanks to which the all-gracious and merciful Lord will allow the humble human being to draw near to the holiness of His presence.

And the wise say, too, that one must not limit oneself to mere knowledge of the deeds of one's *shaikhs*, but grasp through one's heart the sense and significance of those deeds, for they served in their time as the means of attaining Truth.

From the great Naqshbandi [10] *shaikhs* it has come down to us: "Knowing the qualities of *shaikh* predecessors will sometimes be useful to the *murid*, [11] by comparison with his personal observation of them, because the *murid* is at times too worldly, too tied to the earth, and for this reason

---

10   Naqshbandi: followers of Shaikh Bahauddin Naqshband (d. 1389), Muslim religious scholar, founder of the order of the Naqshbandiya at Bukhara.

11   *Murid*: follower, listener, student of the Sufi way; one who submits to the instructions of a *murshid*, or instructor.

there is no benefit if he comes to see in the *shaikhs* that which the Lord gave them from among the gifts of exclusive unity." [12]

The path to God is possible through genuine worship, through suffering and love for the Great and Most High Allah, for only love allows the loving person to improve morally, and only through the assistance of love for one's Lord is the person with a pure heart in a position to surmount the mystical states. But love can be taught only by one who is himself intoxicated by love.

And that person is the noble *shaikh*, a perfect and righteous person. He has walked this path and, thanks to his sincerity and unquestioning service to his own *shaikh*, his steadfast faith, and also the banishing from his soul of all ignoble qualities and the acquisition of noble traits, he has been favored with a degree of the Most High Allah's contemplation.

♦ ♦ ♦

Follow the *shaikhs*, say the wise, discover their noble qualities, and, perhaps, thanks to their blessings, you will one day attain happiness.

---

12 "On the worthiness and laudable qualities of the Sufi Brotherhood of Naqshband and his Path to God," in Shaikh Mukhammad Amin al'-Kurdi al'-Erbili, *The Book of Eternal Gifts* (Russian). Ufa, 2000, p. 7 (author's note).

Sufis say, too, that the seeker must strive to win the love of the *shaikh's* heart, because the hearts of *shaikhs* are the source of divine wisdom, and the *murid*, through the required diligence, sincerity, and loyalty to his teacher, will be enabled to acquire his share of this and, as a result, be honored with the blessedness of their mystical states.

Shaikh Allauddin Attar,[13] may mercy be upon him, said:

> Act in the manner of the great *shaikhs*. You will
> grow sincere and honest in your ways!

♦ ♦ ♦

The life of the incomparable *Hazrat*[14] Bahauddin Naqshband, may his grave be sacred, is an example of the highest service to God, love, and loyalty to his pupils. The story related here was told by the *hazrat* himself.

"Once, in a state of ecstatic attraction to God and immersion in the universe of concealed secrets and disconnection from the world, I left the house, going where my eyes took me. The soles of my feet were pierced by needles. When it began to grow dark, I was drawn to visit Shaikh Sayyid Amir Kulal, may mercy be upon him!

"It was winter and there was a stiff frost. I had noth-

---

13   Allauddin Attar (d. 802): one of Bahauddin's three principle successors.

14   *Hazrat*: respected teacher.

ing on but a short old coat. When I entered his holiness's home, I found him seated amid his associates. He saw me and asked them about me. They told him, and he said, 'Take him from this house!'

"When I left that place, my soul was close to conceiving hatred for the *hazrat* and rising up against him. And it nearly tore from me the bridle of obedience and submission. But the mercy and care of God gradually enveloped me. And I said to myself, 'I shall endure all humiliations in order to deserve the satisfaction of my God. It is that which I cannot do without or escape from.'

"I lay my head down upon the threshold of the *shaikh*'s home and said to myself, 'I will not raise my head, whatever may happen!'

"The snow continued to fall little by little. And I lay on the *shaikh*'s threshold until the day broke. Shaikh Sayyid Amir Kulal,[15] may his grave be sacred, left his house and stepped across my head with his noble foot. When he discovered me, he lifted up my head from the threshold, took me into his house, and gladdened me with joyful news. He said: 'O, my son! The abundance of this joyful news is equal to the measure of your being!'

"Then he began to draw the needles from the soles of my feet with his own noble hands, soothing my wounds and endowing me with his abundant divine revelations and spiritual energy."

---

15 Amir Kulal (d. 1370): Bahauddin's immediate predecessor, who transmitted to him the essentials of the path.

✦ ✦ ✦

The *tariqat* [16] of the Naqshbandi Order—say the great *shaikhs*—is the shortest of all paths that lead the Sufi to the Most High Allah, for the first steps of the *murid* on the mystical path issue from his *shaikh*, who is under the canopy of the spiritual legacy of the Prophet Muhammad, may Allah bless and welcome him, who said: "All that was placed into my breast by Allah, I placed into the breast of Abu Bakr." [17]

This *tariqat* possesses an uninterrupted chain of spiritual continuity known as the *silsila*, which illuminates and reflects the perfection of love among the righteous for God. And in the manifestation of this love—Sufis say—*murids* and *shaikhs* in our *tariqat* are equals. Hazrat Bahauddin Naqshband, may his grave be sacred, said:

> Our *tariqat* is the shortest path to the Most High Allah. And how could it not be the shortest path to Him and connection to Him, if the end of our path is included in its beginning?

May the Most High bless us, too, we *murids*, on the path of moral perfection, and make us sincere followers of the love of our great teachers for God.

---

16   *Tariqat*: spiritual path.

17   *Book of Eternal Gifts*, pp. 8-9 (author's note). Abu Bakr (d. 634): first caliph.

+ + +

A seeker said to Zu'n-nun,[18] "Most of all in the world I want to enter the path of Truth."

Zu'n-nun answered, "You can join our caravan only on two conditions. First, you must do what you do not want to do. Second, you will not be allowed to do what you want. 'Wanting' itself is what stands between man and the path of Truth."

+ + +

The word *murid* means devoted advocate, says the Naqshbandi Shaikh Abdullah Dihlawi,[19] may the mercy of Allah be upon him. The *shaikh* describes how a true *murid* should be:

> He burns with love for Allah, with the desire to
> reach His love. He is bewildered by the love he
> does not know or understand. He cannot sleep or
> make his tears cease. From shame for his past sins
> he cannot lift his face. Whatever he may do, he
> shakes in terror before Allah. He stubbornly strives
> to complete the tasks that will help him to reach
> Allah's love. He is patient and forgiving in all he
> does. In the face of every inconvenience, every dif-
> ficulty, he finds shortcomings in himself. He thinks

18 Zu'n-nun: the Prophet Jonah.
19 Abdullah Dihlawi (d. 1642).

about God with every inward and outward breath. He does not live in forgetfulness (ignorance). He quarrels with no one. He fears causing pain to the heart. He considers hearts the homes of Allah.

Shaikh Allauddin Attar, may mercy be upon him, said:

The *murid* must rely forcefully upon God both externally and internally. The unity of the external and the internal is indispensable.

◆ ◆ ◆

The memory of the founder of the Central Asian school of mysticism, the *Hodjagon*[20] teacher Abdulkhaliq Gizhduvani,[21] may mercy be upon him, is dear to the heart of every mystic or simply spiritual person in our land. The eight fundamental principles he developed were later supplemented by three more from his pupil Bahauddin Naqshband. Together they form the basis of the teachings of the Naqshbandi brotherhood.

According to legend, the father of the future great mystic, the well-known preacher and imam *Hodja*[22] Abduljamil Rumi, had a dream in which Khizr[23] himself revealed that

---

20 *Hodjagon*: school of Central Asian mysticism.

21 Abdulkhaliq Gizhduvani (also Ghujduvani, d. 1179).

22 *Hodja*: title conferred on one descended from the Four Righteous Caliphs; or, one who has made the pilgrimage to Mecca.

23 Khizr: the prophet Elijah.

he would soon set out with a trade caravan from Asia Minor to Bukhara and, after settling in Gizhduvan, have a son whom he would call Abdulkhaliq. And this is indeed what happened. In 1103 Abduljamil Rumi set out with a caravan for Bukhara, and in the settlement of Gizhduvan, as foretold, a son was born, whom he called Abdulkhaliq.

Even as a child, Abdulkhaliq showed phenomenal aptitude for learning. By nine years old, he knew the Qur'an by heart, and by ten he was taking part in the devotions of the Sufis.

Abdulkhaliq studied exegesis with the most learned expert on the Qur'an in Bukhara, the imam Sadruddin,[24] who became his first teacher on the path of divine knowledge. Once Abdulkhaliq read to his teacher the following lines from the Qur'an:

> *Call on your Lord with humility and in private: for*
> *Allah loveth not those who trespass beyond bounds.*[25]

And he asked that it should be made clear.

"If a man remembering God," answered the imam, "performs his *zikr* aloud, if during the *zikr* he should move some part of his body, others will know. And according to the *hadith*, the devil will know too. Here divine knowledge begins, and I am unable to explain more to you. But if God should desire to elucidate this single line, He shall send

24 Sadruddin Qunawi (d. 1274): Sufi theologian, disciple of ibn al-'Arabi.

25 Qur'an 7:55.

down to His chosen one a teacher, who will instruct him completely and provide him with divine knowledge."

Some time after this memorable conversation with Imam Sadruddin, the young man had a dream in which Khizr instructed him in the silent *zikr* and adopted him as his own son.

Abdulkhaliq was twenty-two when in Bukhara he met his future teacher on the mystical path, the famous Yusuf Hamadani, [26] may his grave be holy, and became his *murid*. It is interesting to note that Hazrat Hamadani was himself an advocate of vocal *zikr*, but that was no impediment to his guidance of the young Sufi.

Once Abdulkhaliq told his teacher about his encounter with Khizr and about the methods of silent *zikr* in which the saint had instructed him. The *hodja's* next words opened a path for Abdulkhaliq Gizhduvani for all the rest of his life: "Learning from above is not accorded to every Sufi. But if it is given it must be cared for and cherished, and he should make use of those methods of the *zikr* in which he has been instructed."

Before his death Hodja Yusuf Hamadani took the *khirqa*, or dervish's rag, from his shoulders and placed it upon the shoulders of Abdulkhaliq Gizhduvani.

They say that Yusuf Hamadani served two hundred thirteen *shaikhs* in his time, observed many fast days, journeyed much, and wore a hair shirt. His food was barley

---

26   Yusuf Hamadani (d. 1140). Inaugurated the vein of Sufism in which Bahauddin would become the seventh in a series of Central Asian masters.

bread. He was a boot maker. He gave away his belongings to the poor, orphans, solitary women, and the sick. In the course of his entire life he never asked for alms. He urged his *murids* to work and avoid forbidden foods and fine clothing.

Abdulkhaliq Gizhduvani followed his teacher in everything. His life and teachings are proof of this, the basic theses of which are recounted, in condensed form, in his *Testament*. Dedicated to his son, this thin manuscript speaks of the duties of the Sufi who sets out on the path toward knowledge of God, and places before him a series of essential requirements, whose observance, for the beginning Sufi, are considered mandatory.

The teacher wrote:

"O, my son, to you I bequeath the study of the sciences, the rules of proper behavior and piety, and enjoin you to be God-fearing. Follow in the footsteps of the first righteous Muslims, observe the *sunna*,[27] read works of Muslim law, study the *ahadith* and Qur'anic commentaries.

"Beware of ignorant Sufis; strive always to fulfill your prayers together with others, provided that you are not an imam (leader at prayer) or muezzin.

"Do not covet fame! Verily, fame is a tomb. Be alone among people and do not seek to get hold of some important position ...

"Speak little, eat and sleep still less! Seek solitude. Eat only *halal*.[28]

27 *Sunna*: example or life practice of the Prophet Muhammad.
28 Halal: food permitted by Islamic law.

"Leave behind all desires but the most necessary. It may be that the desire for the earthly will take precedence in you. This desire will destroy your religion and your faith.

"Do not laugh over much, for excessive laughter deadens the heart.

"Insult no one, and do not decorate your exterior, because sprucing oneself up is a sign of one's internal poverty ...

"Do not argue. Ask alms of no one. Do not request the service of others for yourself, rather you yourself serve the *shaikhs* ...

"Do not censure the actions of your *shaikhs* because your censure will gain you nothing.

"Do not be tempted by the earthly world and its inhabitants.

"It is essential that your heart be grieving and sorrowful, your body in ill-health, and your eyes in tears.

"It is essential that your actions be sincere, your prayers full of fear before God, your dress decrepit; that poverty be your companion, Muslim law your sustenance, the mosque your home, the Most High Lord God your interlocutor."

He was an example of service to God. And seeing his perfection, even his enemies could fault him in nothing. In Muhammad Bokir's *Life of Shaikh Naqshband*, the words of Hodja Ali[29] concerning Hazrat Abdulkhaliq Gizhduvani, may his grave be sacred, are cited: "If even one of the followers of Gizhduvani had been standing beside Mansur al-

29   Hodja Ali: *murid* of Abdulkhaliq Gizhduvani.

Halladj,[30] he would not have been executed." This means that even the pupils of Gizhduvani would have been able to convince the prosecutors of Mansur's innocence.

One finds an expression of faith in fate and in providence in the following lines:

> Do not think of tomorrow's food, for with the beginning of the new day the Most High will send you what has been allotted to you.

But this does not mean that one must sit in anticipation of the time when God will send nourishment. It is necessary that one work so that the heavens might send what has been allotted. And no matter hard you try, more than what you have been allotted you shall not receive. No one will eat your portion; no one will take it away. The Most High has determined in eternity the stores of sustenance such that one person would not be able to consume the share of another.

One must not become friends, says Gizhduvani, with those who demonstrate the following five attributes:

- Not considering asceticism as wealth
- Considering an ordinary position as lowly
- Holding out ignorance as knowledge
- Not subjecting their secret and public affairs

---

30 Mansur al-Halladj (d. 922): controversial Persian mystical ascetic, accused of heresy for his statement "I am the truth," imprisoned for eleven years, tortured, and publicly executed.

to account
+ Not fearing the next life.

Human life, says Hazrat Gizhduvani, is too temporal
and illusory for us to become attached to it. Your life is between the inward and outward breath, between light and
darkness. This is why you must strive toward God alone
with every breath you take.

He was tall, with a large head, thick eyebrows, and a
face the color of wheat.

Abdulkhaliq Gizhduvani died in 1179 at the age of
seventy-six. His successor, Bahauddin Naqshband, appeared on the earth nearly one hundred fifty years later. Naqshband saw in a dream his spiritual instructor
Abdulkhaliq Gizhduvani and passed through his spiritual
initiation at Gizhduvani's hands.

+ + +

Still in the time of the Prophet Muhammad, may Allah
bless and welcome him, definite requirements were compiled for *murids*, which were later rewritten by different
orders, but for many centuries practically no changes at
all were permitted. The requirements shown to seekers by
instructors of the *tariqat* were previously quite demanding. For the path of spiritual perfection is a thorny, difficult
path. And God does not, after all, turn everyone over to be
educated by the Sufis.

This path demands that a person apply himself constantly, every minute and every day, and for those who

do not have the will to do so, the Path becomes an insur-
mountable obstacle. When our Shaikh Ibrahim was asked
how many *murids* he had, he replied:

"I do not know. Our teachers forbid us from denying
permission to anyone seeking to be initiated. And we deny
no one. But we neither make nor keep lists of any kind. A
person is initiated, receives a task from us, and after that
might never return again to the *hanaqa*, in which case we
do not guide him along the path. From the fact that this
person was not able to bear the training, we do not suffer
harm, nor does God. The only harm is to the person himself, who displays his weakness of character and of will."

Allah indicates to a person the road to the Sufis, but He
waits for definite effort on the part of His slave.

Shaikh Ibrahim was also asked, "Isn't there a contradic-
tion between the seeker's will during his movement along
the path and his weakness before the will of his *murshid*?"

Shaikh Ibrahim responded:

"The *murid* must come to trust in his *shaikh* completely.
According to a well-known Sufi expression, he must become a 'body in the hands of the cleanser of bodies.' Oth-
erwise, he will learn nothing. It is in carrying out his tasks
independently and alone with the Lord, that he must display diligence and powerful strength of will. Only the strict
observation of the *sunna* of the Prophet Muhammad, may
Allah bless and welcome him, only the consistent performance of tasks, and only the dissolving of the pupil's will in
that of his *shaikh* can be the basis of purifying the seeker's
heart from animal tendencies, aggressions, pettiness, and
the foul fleshly soul."

In the Qur'an it is said:

Man will receive only what he has earned. [31]

May the Most High Allah forgive us our weaknesses and negligence on this path blessed by God.

◆ ◆ ◆

Shaikh Allauddin Attar, may mercy be upon him, used to say:

> Sanctity and subservience are attained only by the man who does not give to his soul power over himself.

How many filthy obstructions must been cleansed from the soul, how many temptations must be overcome, taming one's own ego, which is accustomed to following whims, in order to reach the heart and polish it to a sheen, for only in the pure heart can God take up residence.

Shaikh Bahauddin Naqshband, may his grave be holy, told this story:

"Still at the beginning of my search on the path of mystical knowledge, I met a man from among the lovers of Allah. He was one of the true Sufis. He said to me:

"'You appear to be one of the zealots.'

"I responded, 'I hope that I shall become a true zealot,

---

31 Qur'an 53:40.

thanks to a glance of mercy from the lovers of God.'

"He asked, 'How do you pass your time?'

"I said, 'If I find some food, I thank God. If not, I am patient.'

"He smiled and said, 'That is not difficult. The important thing is to place labors upon the soul. This is how it is done. If you have no food for an entire week, do not allow your soul to grumble, but let it be at peace.'

"I came near to him and asked his help. He commanded me to practice the suppression and restraint of my desires, care for the week, powerless, and crippled, with whom other people do not trouble themselves, noting in particular that I should display submissiveness, obedience, and self-abasement.

"I began to fulfill his command and proceeded, as the holy saint had ordered, over the course of many days.

"After that he commanded me to render service to all the animals, to heal them of their various wounds and sores, with utmost effort and obligingness.

"I burdened myself with this labor and did all that he had ordered me to do, and if a dog came across my path, I would stop so that it should pass first, not wishing to overtake it. Thus did six years pass.

"Then he ordered me to render service unto the dogs of the nearest neighborhood and to request help from the animals. He said, 'You will lower yourself to the state of a dog. And, serving dogs, you will attain happiness and be deserving of great reward.'

"I spared nothing in fulfilling this task, obeying his command and desiring to attain his joyful prediction. And once, meeting a dog on my way, I suddenly fell into the most profound mystical state. I stopped before the dog and was seized by powerful tears. Right there the dog too fell onto its back and raised its four legs to the sky. I heard its pitiful sighs and mournful moaning. I raised my hands in humility and obedience and said, 'Amen!' and the dog grew quiet and raised itself to its paws.

"One of those same days, wandering on the outskirts of Bukhara, I found a chameleon, immersed with all its being in contemplation of the sun's beauty. I looked with wonder at the chameleon, and the passionate desire to ask it to show me mercy and compassion took hold of my soul.

"The chameleon still remained in place. I stood up before it in a posture of the fullest respect and civility and raised my hands. The chameleon came out of its immersion in considering the sun's beauty and fell onto its back, turning toward the sky. And I said, 'Amen!'

"After this the man commanded me to practice clearing roads of refuse and rubbish. For six long years I demonstrated stubbornness and perseverance in this difficult work. No one ever saw the sleeves or hem of my shirt free from the dust and dirt of the road. All this, and the other tasks my instructor ordered me to fulfill, I fulfilled conscientiously, sincerely, and without murmur. From it all I discovered a beneficial influence on my soul and an unprecedented improvement in my mystical states."

+ + +

The path of the Sufi is the path of perfecting the soul, which is impossible without taming and reeducating his self-loving *nafs*.[32] The *nafs* is nourished by the earthly and animal passions, and, driven by base desires, a man forgets about God. His soul ceases to be capable of compassion, and ever more place inside it is given over to the transient, earthly passions, which he is not able to satisfy.

Even having attained his goal, man is disappointed then and there, for his *nafs* is insatiable. It supplants the divine principle in him and fills the soul with base passions, and in the pursuit of satisfying these, he wastes his life, which invariably ends for him in the profoundest disillusionment.

The Sufi reeducates his *nafs*, forcing it to be docile, obedient and quiet, meek. But how much sweat must pour, how much suffering be endured, so that one day the *nafs* might acknowledge that it is obedient to its master.

◆ ◆ ◆

Shaikh Ubaydullah Ahrar Vali,[33] may his grave be sacred, told the following story:

"In Samarqand I settled at the school of Qutbuddin Sadri. There I found four men sick with fever. I undertook to serve them, washing their clothes and cleaning their personal belongings. Through excessive exertion I myself

---

32 *Nafs*: "I," the self, the ego, the carnal soul (author's note).
33 Ubaydullah Ahrar Vali (d. 1490): influential Sufi teacher whose disciples spread over Iran, Turkey, India, and Arabia.

came down with fever. Somehow in the night, shivering with fever, I managed to fetch four pitchers of water and washed their clothes and rugs.

"And when I was in Herat, I went to the bathing hut of Abdullah Ansari and served the people there by giving massages. I served without distinguishing between free man or slave, rich or poor. One day I gave massages to sixteen visitors to the bath, nor did I take anything from them for my efforts."

＋ ＋ ＋

The *shaikhs* of the Naqshbandiya knew the price of the time allotted them by God and filled every passing moment with that which was required by it. They engaged in the fulfillment of their *zikr* only when no one needed their services.

If a Muslim desires to render service unto another, honor him!—say the *shaikhs*. For service to another is the reason for God's acceptance of hearts and the condition for crossing over to the *zikr* and *murakaba*.[34] Some people suppose that saying additional prayers or fasting more is better and more useful than the demonstration of service to one's neighbors. But that is not the case.

The result of rendering service is love and the attachment of hearts, because service is by its very nature based upon love for those who are more deserving of it. And this is what differentiates the fruits of a Sufi's recitation of

34 *Murakaba*: the contemplation of God in one's heart.

additional prayers from the fruits of a Sufi's service to others .... In accordance with the scale of the love you demonstrate to others, the Most High's love will come to you in return.

Therefore have the *shaikhs* of the Naqshbandi *tariqat*, may mercy be upon them, yearned to serve others but not make use of others' service to them.

♦ ♦ ♦

The Sufi's path is the path of compassion, love, and generosity, for the Most High himself is compassion, generosity, and love. God is perfection itself, and to be in love with Him means to perfect one's soul such as to see the beautiful in everything. But years of sincere and tireless service to the Lord must pass, the lover must shed rivers of tears, forcing the body and soul to suffer, before one's eyes will learn to see the beautiful and one's tongue to speak with sincerity.

♦ ♦ ♦

Shaikh Bahauddin, may his grave be sacred, said:

"In the expulsion of devilish incitements and evil desires from their souls, the *salikun*[35] may be divided into three groups:

"The Sufi who represents the first group sees evil desires and engages in expelling them until they enter into him.

"The Sufi who represents the second group expels the

---

35   *Salikun* (sg. *salik*): Sufis at the start of their study.

devilish desires until they have entered his soul, settling there and taking firm root.

"The Sufi who represents the third group is he who, after the evil desires have grown strong within his soul, attempts to distance them and drive them from himself, though without being completely successful in his efforts."

"But it must be noted that if the *salik* learns the place of origin of these desires and the reason for their striving toward him, then success and benefit will not pass him by."

✦ ✦ ✦

The path of the righteous is the path of civility, nobility, and a person's soulful beauty. Shaikh Bahauddin Naqshband, may mercy be upon him, has said:

"There are three codes of civility and conduct in our *tariqat*:

"First, the *adab* [36] relating to the Great and Almighty Allah, in accordance with which the *murid* is fully prepared both externally and internally for bowing down to God, following His prescriptions, shunning that which He has forbidden, and refusing with all his being everything except the Lord God.

"Second, the *adab* in relation to the Messenger of Allah, may Allah bless and welcome him. For this the Sufi must plunge into a state of interpretation of the Prophet Muhammad's injunction to Muslims: 'Conduct yourself in

---

36   *Adab*: a code of rules for proper behavior, etiquette.

life and religion according to my prescriptions and com-
mandments.'

"Third, the *adab* in relation to the *shaikhs*. This consists
of the need for the *murid* to follow the *shaikhs*, obeying
them in everything, in as much as this will serve as the
basis and means of observing the injunctions bequeathed
to Muslims by the Prophet Muhammad, may Allah bless
and welcome him! The *shaikhs* have attained a degree that
allows them rightfully to call upon the Lord God. Therefore the *murid* must follow with care the mystical states of
his *shaikhs*, imitate their states, and keep to the image of
their life."

✦ ✦ ✦

In his book *Adab as-salikhin* (Etiquette of the Righteous), Muhammad Sadyki-i-Kashgari [37] brought together
and set forth with strict consistency the rules of politeness of the righteous that most closely correspond to the
example of the Prophet Muhammad, may Allah bless and
welcome him.

Let us, too, attempt to retrace the most important of
these and, with the permission of Allah and my own
Shaikh Ibrahim, may mercy be upon him, express the
point of view of other well-known and lesser known mem-
bers, past and present, of the *tariqat*. May Allah forgive

---

37   Muhammad Sadyki i-Kashgari (also Sadik Kaxkari): eighteenth-
century Uyghur scholar.

me if I, *bechora*, [38] express my own, perhaps, not completely faithful viewpoint on certain points of the Sufi's behavior, so that the mistakes I have made might be avoided by others.

38 *Bechora*: Uzbek word meaning wretch, poor devil.

Part One

Observations on the Gathering

On Sitting at a Distance

The *murid* who has come to his *pir*[39] must seat himself at a distance from him.

Passage along the spiritual path is called *sayr wa-suluk*[40]; it demands deep deliberation, insight and diligent observation of each instant of life from the person who has accepted the *baiyat*.[41]

It is said in the Qur'an:

> *And those who strive for Us, we shall guide them in Our paths.*[42]

I received confirmation of these words from the blessed lips of our Shaikh Ibrahim, who once said in conversation, "You think it was your friend or acquaintance who brought you to the *hanaqa*? You are mistaken, for it was God who took pity on you, having seen your humble desire to serve Him. The Merciful One saw the tiniest spark of love that might be ignited such that your soul should truly become God-fearing and meek.

"There are many in the world who have wanted to

---

39 *Pir*: elder, head of the order of dervishes; spiritual instructor.
40 *Sayr wa-suluk*: the spiritual path or journey (*sayr*) and the methods (*suluk*) for proceeding along it.
41 *Baiyat*: initiation into Sufism.
42 Qur'an 29:69.

traverse the path of spiritual perfection, but God does not show them the way to the *hanaqa* and does not give them into the hands of the Sufis to be educated. Such people read spiritual books, converse with the wise, and finally, thinking they have mastered the subject, themselves write about dervishes and Sufism. But as long as the Most High does not grant permission, the way to the Sufis is barred to them. For this reason give thanks to the Lord God upon every inward and every outward breath, that He has guided you to the *hanaqa* in the bosom of love.

"The Most High saw in your soul the need for spiritual perfection and your displeasure with yourself. Until the need for God appears in our soul, He will not love us. The Messenger of Allah, may Allah bless and welcome him, said: 'My glory comes from spiritual poverty. I have been glorified above the other prophets because I was gifted with poverty of spirit.' It is imperative that you and I feel in our souls such spiritual poverty ..." (here the *hazrat*'s voice broke off, and his eyes filled with tears) "... so that the Merciful One might then allow us to approach the understanding of God and the consciousness of His greatness."

+ + +

During the initiation into Sufism, the *shaikh* pronounces ritual phrases that end with the following words:

"Now you enter the world of love and meekness. Do you repent of your previous sins?"

"I repent!" answers the initiate.

"And we also repent. And from this moment," continues the *shaikh*, "you become pure as a newborn babe …."

✦ ✦ ✦

Movement along the path is perfection of one's civility, perfection of one's "I," its reeducation to the point that it becomes civil and learns humility, such that it will not then hinder a person from serving God.

The Sufi's civility manifests itself in his relation to the Holy Book, from which he reads *surahs*,[43] heedless of the abundant tears that roll down his cheeks; in his relation to the *shaikh*, before whom he experiences constant spiritual trepidation; in his relation to the people who surround him and for whom he is prepared to give his life.

Civility is not simply a respectful orientation to all that surrounds you, it is attentiveness and sensitivity multiplied by respect and compassion for your neighbor. It is, in the end, reverence for everything created by the Compassionate and Most Gracious Allah.

From civility emerges the insight that signifies choice of the only correct decision, the only correct thought, the only correct movement of the soul and body upon each instant issued by God and sanctified by Him.

Insight and consciousness are blood brothers. And here, slave of God that I am, having strayed in the darkness of

43 *Surah* (also *sura*): one of the one hundred fourteen chapters in the Qur'an.

my life, for some unknown services before God, I find myself brought before Him in the *hanaqa* and given into the hands of the Sufis, so that they may teach me the civility of the righteous.

Consciousness is impossible without insight, and without consciousness of oneself and others it is impossible to be insightful. Being conscious each instant that God sees you, hears you, and feels; understanding that you have no right to display carelessness in anything—this means believing that your insightfulness, your relation to God, the degree of your fear before Him and the depth of your love for Him are worthy of improvement.

Shaikh Bahauddin Naqshband, may mercy be upon him, said, "Nothing brings as much benefit to the Sufi at the start of his path than diligence, self-abasement, and increased striving. Keeping to these alone, I was favored by being noted by God."

God Willing

One young Sufi had a neighbor who came to him repeatedly to express his readiness to enter the path of the *tariqat* and asked to be taken to the Sufi's *shaikh*.

"Fine," answered the devout neighbor. "If God should so choose, next time I am preparing to go to the *hanaqa*, I will let you know."

Some time passed, and the dervish was preparing to

visit his *shaikh*. On the eve of his departure, he went to his neighbor and told him of his intention.

"This is rather sudden," complained his neighbor. "I have so many things to do. And I have a family to feed."

"He who has less of the world is the richest in the world," said the dervish, closing the door behind him.

More time passed. The dervish was again preparing to go to the *hanaqa*, and he went to his neighbor.

"Could we put off the visit to the *shaikh* for a week?" asked the neighbor, again grieved.

"No, we cannot," answered the Sufi, "because the soul in which God is to be born must distance itself from time, but in you that which is of fleeting importance reigns. Take care of your business. Apparently that has been ordained for you from on high. God does not want to give you to the Sufis."

❖ ❖ ❖

All the brothers with whom I have spoken acknowledge that before entering the *hanaqa* they feel a particular anxiety that is incomparable with any other in their life. Let me share, slave of God and *bechora* that I am, the sensations my soul experiences as soon as it learns of my intention to visit the *shaikh*.

Two whole days before setting out, my soul, like a sapling frightened by the first frost, grows stiff and rigid. Life, which up to then has had a certain rhythm connected to earning one's daily bread and other such cares, suddenly and unexpectedly slows, and all earthly cares recede into the distance: I can no longer think of anything but the journey.

I see before me the *hanaqa* and my beloved *shaikh*, at the very remembrance of whom my soul trembles, and tears well up in my eyes.

The most frightening part begins on the day of the journey, when all the instants of life between my last visit to the *hanaqa* and today's turn over in my mind; I recall all my sins and unrighteous words and deeds. The thought that my *shaikh* knows about all my inadequacies pierces through me like an electric current; he reads all my sinful thoughts, and for that reason there is no avoiding my shame before him.

While still at home, having performed my ablutions and read the corresponding prayer of the *shukru-vuzu'*, I slowly finger each prayer bead, reading the *Astagfirullah*, and then the *surah 'Al-Fatiha* once through and the *Al'-Ihlas* three times through, and I give thanks to my *shaikh* for what I have read. Thus did teachers of the past advise one to proceed, and thus do experienced Sufis of today advise.

As I approach the *hanaqa*, I feel my heartbeat quicken, as anxiousness takes hold of my entire body and my legs grow wooden. Shame awaits you, I reprimand myself. How many sins you have brought down on your poor head since last seeing your *shaikh*!

Yes, of course, I say. All this time the spirit of my teacher has followed me everywhere and managed to drive away evil thoughts as soon as the image of my incomparable *shaikh* rose up before me. His gracious spirit has accompanied each of my steps, capturing each of my thoughts, watching over every one of my actions, like a young mother anxiously observing the first steps of her first-born child, ready to support him at any moment and, if he should fall, help him to stand again.

As soon as my hands or feet are preparing to commit some unseemly deed and a sinful thought visits my consciousness, I call my *shaikh* to my aid, and his image immediately appears before my eyes and saves me.

He is not only inside me, my *shaikh*, he is everywhere and in everything, in every face I meet in my frequent travels. He is in every object, every thing. And he sees me as I sit, rest, and walk. He watches after me with reproach if I am negligent in prayer.

Our teacher Hodja Ubaydullah Ahrar Vali has said:

> The thoughts of the *murid* are found between the brows of the *murshid*.

And now I enter the *hanaqa* and see our *hazrat* and no longer remember anything or see anyone. The passing glance of my *shaikh*, directed at me, evokes discomposure and fascination. I almost do not see the face of my *shaikh*, that beautiful, enlightened face, emanating mercy and light, melting inside me.

Or rather no, it is I who have melted inside the *shaikh*, and each word he pronounces rumbles like a mountain echo within me, such that I cease to notice the involuntary tears that have filled my eyes. It is not a simple emotion, it is the utter purity of his soul overflowing into mine; it is a great height over mountains and fields above which my soul floats like vapor, inspired by the mountainous purity and freshness.

As if sensing my state, which is not far removed from one who has fainted, our *hazrat* turns to me. Smiling as always, he asks in a gentle voice about my loved ones and my unfinished house.

I sit with my head lowered and do not dare look. But I feel him, guess his movements, and he need only look in my direction for me to turn to him in an instant, with a slight start, like a bird grown stiff on a branch, and be ready to catch every word he might pronounce.

It is surprising that he remembers the names of all the *murids*, knows all their problems, and never lets slip an occasion to support each one. His word, even just one of his words, gives me such strength that, remembering it long after, I walk as if with wings.

On Listening Attentively

One must listen attentively to the instructions of one's *pir*, imprint his words on one's heart, and attempt to follow them.

On this subject the Messenger of Allah, may Allah bless and welcome him, pronounced the following *hadith*: "Luqman instructed his son with these words:

"'Consider it necessary to sit with the learned and listen attentively to the words of the community's wise, for it is through the light of wisdom that Allah brings dead hearts to life, just as He brings dead earth to life with abundant rain. And no one knows religion better than the wise.'"

It is said in the Qur'an:

> O ye who believe, fear Allah, and be among the truthful. [44]

Shaikh Akbar, [45] may mercy be upon him, said:

> If in your dealings you do not submit to the desires
> of others, you will never be able to rid yourself
> of the desires of the passions, even if you should
> spend your entire life trying. Therefore, should you

44   Qur'an, 9:119.
45   Shaikh al-Akbar ibn Arabi (d. 1240): celebrated Muslim mystic philosopher.

meet a person to whom you cultivate an attachment in your heart, look after him and follow his instructions as though you have no will of your own and no desires are left to you.

Muhammad Parsa,[46] may his grave be made holy with light, writes the following in the *Treatise on Holiness*:

"Through the constant elimination of willful motives, diverse natural desires, and the distancing from oneself of the traits and signs of the human essence, the slave makes progress along the steps toward God, until at last he reaches the summit of freedom from the will and truly abandons all desires.

"Only then, having raised himself from the depth of human nature to the utmost height of perfection of true God-worship, is he suitable to be elevated, through the transformative and all-submissive divine foundation, to the level of the disappearance of self within God and being with Him ....

"This happiness becomes possible after the disappearance of the qualities of human nature and the attainment of true absence of will, such that in both worlds of the seeker there is no desire and no goal other than Him. And true absence of will arrives through the denial of one's own will and the surrender of oneself into the complete direction of the *shaikh*.

"Subordination to the will of the *shaikh* is a ladder leading to submission to (divine) predestination and predeter-

46   Muhammad Parsa (d. 1420): successor of Bahauddin Naqshband.

mination. If he successfully copes with the first, then he will succeed in the second as well. Only when he succeeds in submitting to the transformative power of the *shaikh* will the heavy veil concealing the beauty of Truth fall down before him. Then will the aspirant attain the cherished, the seeker—his goal."[47]

♦ ♦ ♦

Protecting me like a mother bird protects its still senseless chick, one experienced Sufi explained the significance of the *shaikh* in the fate of a person who has started out on the path to the attainment of Truth in the following manner:

"Imagine that our *pir*, may mercy be upon him, is a powerful electric station connected to the divine supply source. It receives as much of the sacred energy as it is capable of holding, with the help of God, to illuminate the road for thousands and thousands of wayward people like you and me.

"To each of us is given exactly that amount of energy that we are capable of passing through our hearts. If lines that are intended for a certain amount of energy are given greater load, they burn out. In our negligence, we do not over exert ourselves such as to increase the capacity of our conduits, or work hard through long nighttime sittings in prayer to God, and we receive exactly the amount that we have earned.

47   Muhammad Parsa, *Treatise on Holiness*, in *Wisdom of the Sufis* (Russian). Saint Petersburg, 2001, pp. 308, 310 (author's note).

"It is not our desires that increase the quantity of energy advanced to us from the *hazrat*, it is our efforts. We must feel constant need, hunger, for the divine energy, and then the conduits along with it comes to us from our *hazrat*, may the mercy of Allah be upon him, will be widened further and further. The accumulated energy, some time, thanks to our patience, effort, and love for God, will also help us, God willing, to shine the light of Truth even on our souls, lingering in the dark."

My feet had gone to sleep, and I tried to stretch them slightly before me. The *murid* sitting next to me was listening attentively to the brother who was speaking. He glanced at my feet and indicated with his face that they were pointed in the direction of the *qibla*, Mecca. I was ready to sink through the earth from shame, and I instantly drew them in and lowered my head. The brother, having given us instructions, also noticed my awkwardness but pretended that he hadn't. I was extremely thankful to him for this, but my attention was scattered: my cheeks continued to burn with shame, and it was all I could do to try and concentrate once more on the discussion.

The brother continued, "If we are slow to rise for nighttime prayers and limit ourselves to a small number of *zikrs*, loving sleep more, then that is enough for Allah to omit us from his mercy that night. I am surprised at the generosity of our *hazrat*. Each time we come to the *hanaqa*, he magnanimously enriches us with divine energy, which we then waste without a thought. And then, exhausted and weak, our heads lowered with guilt, we come back to our *hazrat* and again he shares divine mercy with us."

The time for evening prayer was approaching, and the *murids* began to get up in order to renew their ablutions.

When I left the room, the brother who had made me a side remark during the discussion, stopped me:

"Don't get distracted by what you're doing now. Think rather what Allah will do with you, and then everything will fall into place. When we remember that Allah sees us, we already begin to avoid mistakes."

I suddenly recalled the words of Hazrat Alisher Navoi,[48] may mercy be upon him, who says in one of his lesser known texts:

> *They said, too, that our teaching is discussion. And glory lies in solitude, in poverty. Pious is that society that finds itself in discussion. It is the condition of being attentive to one another. The All High thus ordained that those well versed in Sufism should conduct discussions. Until death itself. . . . And in that its abundance will be found.*[49]

The feeling of displeasure with oneself, our *hazrat* had said that very morning, is a good feeling, but it cannot all by itself transform what we do daily into satisfaction. For that one must work a great deal and with stubborn persistence, remembering that God worries more over us than we do over ourselves.

---

48   Alisher Navoi, also Ali-Shir Nava'i (1441-1501): Central Asian poet.
49   "Hodja Bahauddin," in *Star of the East* (Russian), No. 11-12, p. 123 (author's note).

Allah has bestowed on each of us, he said, a determinate quantity of breaths. Those we have performed without remembering the name of our Most High Lord in our hearts have quitted our hearts irrevocably, leaving nothing but emptiness behind. But the inward breath in which the name of God was present has made us richer, for it has filled us with Divine energy.

On Choosing the Opportune Moment to Speak

Before entering into conversation with the *pir*, one must make absolutely certain that the *shaikh* has time available and not thrust conversation upon him inopportunely. When an opportune moment to speak arises, one should state briefly, to the best of one's ability, what one wants to say.

How many times have I seen for myself that for a newly initiated *murid* who asks a question of the *hazrat*, the important thing is not to hear the answer but to find some hidden praise in it, like a sign of encouragement for his hidden abilities or knowledge. And it has happened that he received such encouragement and grew calm, pleased with himself and the fact of his presence in the *hanaqa* among the Sufis.

But often such partial encouragement has acted upon certain *murids* in a weakening manner, and afterwards it was not possible to hold them back. They went on talking, and the *shaikh* sat silently, listening in respect. As always it was the experienced *murids* who could not stand it and, unobserved by the *shaikh*, would poke the speaker carried away by his own words in the ribs, until his voice suddenly cut out.

I myself passed through this, slave and *bechora* that I am, and the memory of my former self-confidence alone is enough to make me blush with shame even now.

Bury Your Intellect

One man whose wife had died devoted himself to Sufism and, since he had no relatives or children, with the permission of his *shaikh* he moved into the *hanaqa*. He was a curious man and liked to ask questions. He had another especially distinguishing trait: without waiting for the end of the answer, he would begin to revise his question, adding and complicating it so that, in the end, he wore down everyone with his tiresomeness.

More than once the experienced *murids* told him that one did not pose questions in the *hanaqa*, one only received answers. But it was useless: for a while the *murid* would be able to keep silent, but then he would break in again.

A year passed before the man understood that he would receive much more by preserving silence than by asking questions. And so he was quiet, but the questions kept accumulating in his heart.

Once when he was sitting apart, the *shaikh* approached him and asked quietly, "Are you still asking questions?"

"Yes!" answered the embarrassed *murid*, jumping up.

"As long as you are asking questions and answering them yourself, you'll attain nothing."

"What can I do?" asked the *murid*, disconcerted.

"Go to the grave of your wife in the cemetery," responded the Sufi. "Bury your intellect next to your wife's grave and let it be calmed there."

Yearn for God

A man came to a Sufi and began telling him at length, and in exhausting detail, about his beggarly life, about his children who had stopped listening to him, about his wife spending out of all measure, even what he had managed to earn with great difficulty, and about the many other problems that rained down upon him.

The Sufi nodded, maintaining his usual silence. At last the man grew tired of speaking about himself and his own misfortunes and grew quiet, waiting for a commiserating or sympathetic response.

But the Sufi was silent, plunged in meditation.

Again the man broke the silence, addressing the Sufi with a request: "There are rumors about you," said the man tentatively. "They say you possess divine mercy. Desire it for me as well, so that God might take pity on wretched me."

"I cannot," answered the dervish.

"Why?" asked the man in genuine surprise.

"Because in my own twenty years of service to the Lord, it is unlikely that I have merited God's favor."

"So the people extol you in vain?" asked the stranger.

"Absolutely in vain," agreed the Sufi.

"What am I to do?" asked the man in dismay.

"Yearn for God."

"I have no yearning in my heart," said the man, throwing out his hands.

"A true pity," answered the Sufi. "Yearn for yearning then with all your soul, and maybe, with time, yearning will arise in your heart."

On Gentle Words

In conversing with the *murshid* one must pronounce one's words quietly and gently.

Soft-heartedness is one of the main traits of those who bow their heads in obedience before God. The following story is related in the *hadith* passed on to at-Tabrani.[50] Djarir,[51] peace be unto him, tells of how the Prophet, may Allah bless and welcome him, said, "The recompense Allah gives for soft-heartedness He does not give for foolhardiness; and when Allah comes to love one from among his slaves, He implants softness of heart within him."

◆ ◆ ◆

And the Prophet, may Allah bless and welcome him, also said:

> Be as guests in the world. Choose mosques as you select living places. Train your hearts in gentleness. Be diligent in your thoughts and tears.

◆ ◆ ◆

---

50   At-Tabrani: wrote *al-Mu'jam al-Kabir*, source of *ahadith*.
51   Abu Dja'far Muhammad Djarir al-Tabari (d. 923): historian of Islam, exegete of the Qur'an.

One never speaks loudly in the *hanaqa*. Even during conversation there is an impression that a halo of silence suspends above the room and the beneficent angels who circle above it are blessing the Sufis seated there. Silence, as if there is no ceiling, it has melted into the sky. Silence, as if the walls have opened to the horizon. And you are like a blade of grass in the steppe, alone with God, your senses overflowing.

It is surprising that no matter how many *murids* may come, they all find space within the small confines of the room and no one is left beyond the threshold.

The *shaikh* enters and the coolness of silence emanates from him. Even when he speaks.

Be seated beside the Sufi, my soul. Melt in his quiet words, from which flows boundlessness, eternity both near and far.

On Obtaining Counsel

One must not undertake anything without the counsel of the *pir*, even if compelled by the most urgent necessity.

Many times have I seen for myself how important it is to receive the blessing of one's *shaikh* before beginning anything. Once in the *hanaqa* I even heard a *shaikh* say, "Without concurrence with me, my *murids* cannot even drive in a nail."

I thought for a long time about these words of the *hazrat* until it became clear that the most important thing was of course not in the hammer or in striking the nail. It was in the fact that this was how the *murid* who relied only on the Lord and his *pir* acted.

A Desert Crossing

Two young Sufis were faced with a long, exhausting journey across the desert. Just before setting out, as is proper on such occasions, they went to their *hazrat* in order to ask his permission.

The *shaikh* gave them his blessing and pronounced a prayer in parting:

"May he who remembers us be remembered by the Most High!"

One of the two *murids* was physically strong and hoped to overcome the desert with ease. Laughing, he clapped his frailer companion on the shoulder and said with self-as-surance that he would not leave him behind in his hour of need.

For the first few days the brawny man held up cheerfully and even tried to make fun of the taciturn concentration of his companion, who slowly moved forward, immersed in his own thoughts.

But then the water ran out, and the grueling heat began to sap the travelers' last strength. Now the *murid* who had expected to playfully overcome the desert began to fall behind. His companion, it seemed, did not notice the heat at all: dropping his chin to his chest, just as at the beginning of their road, he slowly continued without stopping even once.

A day later, when a third of the passage still remained, a head wind began to blow. The burning wind swept up the sand from the travelers' feet, blinding the men and slow-ing their already sluggish progress still further. The brawny fellow was the first to succumb to the strain. He fell down, covered his head with the skirt of his quilt robe, and lay still—he had no strength to go on.

Some time later the second Sufi approached and held out a flask with water to his companion.

"Where did you get the water," the brawny fellow asked feebly in surprise. "We finished our water a long time ago, didn't we?"

"I don't know," answered the Sufi in all honesty. "I take a few gulps from the flask, but each time it fills up again with cool water."

The brawny man was still more surprised and could not

take his amazed eyes from the flask. He had already drunk his fill but simply could not believe his companion's words and again put his lips to the flask. In truth it had again filled with the cool, intoxicating liquor. When he returned the empty flask to his neighbor, again came the sound of gurgling, flowing liquid.

The brawny fellow grabbed his own flask and, crying out, tossed it aside. The empty flask had grown hot under the merciless desert sun and burned his fingers.

The thin Sufi carried his exhausted companion on his back the remainder of the way.

But they finished their passage, time passed, and again the travelers came to the *hanaqa*.

The *shaikh* inquired graciously about the health of his *murids* and said, "We tried as well as we could to support you on the road, but the strong *murid* turned away."

"I recalled with my mind," said the brawny man, lowering his head guiltily, "that you were helping us, but then doubt crept into my soul, and I hadn't enough strength left to remember you."

"I was so afraid of letting you fall from my heart that I didn't notice the hardships," responded the thin *murid*, but he couldn't go on: tears of gratitude had welled up in his eyes.

On Avoiding Pleasantries

One must not make jokes or witty remarks while speaking with a *shaikh*. Nor should one joke with others in the *shaikh's* presence: it is best not to talk at all without his permission.

"For three years," confessed one young *murid*, "I came to our *hazrat* in the *hanaqa*, listened to his wise council, and didn't feel any change inside. But once I arrived as usual and overheard the *shaikh* addressing his *murids* with sorrow:

"'Each time before sending you out onto the road, I place you on the backs of fleet-footed racers, and each time you come back, hanging your heads and holding on by the horses' tails.'

"'I must remember God more,' I thought, ashamed of my carelessness and sloth. And I understood, too, that I must forget about myself.

"'How can one forget about oneself?' asked a young *murid*, still not grasping what the more experienced brother was getting at.

"'If you are conscious of yourself seated in the *hanaqa* among the Sufis,' answered the brother, 'then you have missed half of what the teacher was saying on this subject. And if you heard all of what others have said about it, then you have missed all the rest.'

"'What can one do?' asked the young *murid*.

"'Be a silent, fallen leaf, defenseless, helpless, and without will, carried away by the autumn wind into the unknown distance.... Only then will you recall everything that the *hazrat* says.'"

+ + +

If as a result of profound silence tears do not well up in the eyes of the murid, *it means he was not silent on God's account.*

+ + +

The *hanaqa* is the place where one suddenly becomes conscious of the senselessness of the stream of words that fell from one's mouth before.... Slowly that water begins to flow into sand, the scalding sand of the desert, which can never be filled with words....

The *hanaqa* is the place where your life slows down, just, it seems, so that you might grow ashamed of earlier days.

The *hanaqa* is the place where each word of the *shaikh* is a saving swallow of water amid that very same desert of life.

Shoulders tremble just perceptibly from silent weeping. It is the soul cleansing itself of all that has been blocked up by words, iridescent like inflated balloons that, bursting, turn to emptiness.

The *hanaqa* is the place where a person becomes aware of his sins.

+ + +

According to the testimony of Anas,[52] may mercy be upon him, who said, "I heard the Messenger of Allah, may Allah bless and greet him, say, 'Allah the Almighty said,'

> O son of Adam, for as long as you continue to appeal to Me and call upon me with prayers, I shall forgive you for what you have done without worry. O son of Adam, even if your sins should reach unto the clouds of the sky and you ask forgiveness of Me, I shall forgive you. O son of Adam, if you should come to Me with sins whose greatness is equal to the earth and appear before Me and blame no other, I shall grant you forgiveness of equal measure.[53]

✦ ✦ ✦

A *shaikh* entered a room where two young dervishes were seated, greeted everyone, and sat down in his usual place. Everyone thought that now a conversation would begin and glanced now and then at their teacher. But he was silent. Lowering his head slightly, he sat immersed in contemplation and resembled an eagle carved out of mountain stone. At last he slowly raised his head and said, "Silence without reflection is hypocrisy with rosary beads

52   Malik ibn Anas al-Ashabi (d. 795): author of oldest surviving compendium on Islamic law, compiler of the *ahadith* of Muhammad, his Companions and followers.
53   Cited by at-Tirmidhi (d. 892): Arab scholar and author of one of the canonical compilations of *ahadith*.

in your hands. Better to babble incessantly than remain silent in such a manner.

"Your silence," he said, turning to one of the dervishes, "is like a fragile sapling on a windless day: shameful, shy, without confidence. The first little breeze will dislodge your timid leaves, and any external thought will destroy your silence.

"Your silence," he said, turning to the other dervish, "is heavy like autumn water, weighed upon by your wordlessness. A light rock that falls from the bank will disturb the water's smooth surface and leave no trace of the heaviness behind.

"Be a stone when you contemplate. The stone, it neither hears nor sees. Nor does it feel itself contemplating. It does not remember that it is a stone. It is a part of Divine Truth."

The Sufi stopped speaking and sank once more into silence. The beads he had been telling before went stiff in his hand, so that it was not at all clear where the beads ended and his hand began.

On Avoiding Boastfulness

One must not try and show off one's knowledge or erudition in the presence of a *shaikh*.

Those who sit beside their *shaikh* and want to show their own learning and erudition, say the wise, are not rewarded with blessedness or mercy. Only the man who comes to his *shaikh* with an empty heart will return from him with a full one.

They say, too, that one must not go to the *shaikh* in order to see miracles performed, for such is not a criterion for determining a *shaikh*'s level. And if indeed someone were to think up the notion of going to a *shaikh* in order to test him, that person would come away devoid of happiness.

Many times I have seen beginning *murids* trying with all their might to show off before their *hazrat*. At least some have limited themselves to posing questions; others by contrast have begun to discourse on Sufism itself to the *shaikh*.

And the most surprising part is that the *hazrat* has not once interrupted these conceited dare-devils, who've taken the liberty of telling the master about the path, while this servant has burned from shame at their tactless, naïve simplicity. But in the end, for many such self-confident people everything turns out well. After six months many of them become as silent and obedient as lambs. And at the slightest memory of their past self-confidence, they break into a sweat. I say this of myself as well.

I Do Not Know

A Sufi sat before his house and answered questions put to him by passersby. In all the surrounding area he was considered a wise, insightful man. Most surprising was the fact that he called himself ignorant, and his wife was of the same opinion.

And here thirty people passed by today and asked him thirty questions. And to all thirty questions the Sufi answered with sincere sorrow, "I don't know."

In the evening his curious wife, having listened through the window to these many questions and answers, came and began to reprimand him:

"I always suspected you were a little stupid. You couldn't even answer the simplest questions they asked. So how is it the people didn't thrash you?"

"I don't understand either," confessed the Sufi in all sincerity.

"And why was it," asked his wife, unwilling to leave off, "that you answered simply, 'I don't know' and the people went away satisfied and only the last one, hearing your answer, covered his face with his hands?"

"Twenty-nine of them," answered the Sufi, "knew the answer before asking me the question, so my not knowing reinforced their self-affirmation, and that's why they went away satisfied."

"And the last one? What question did he ask you?"

"Who fears God more, he asked, the man who speaks or the man who keeps silent?"

"I don't know," I said to him. "And he broke into tears."

+ + +

The clever man comes to the *hanaqa* in order to place his will into the hands of the perfect one to whom he has given his hand.[54]

The stupid man comes to the *hanaqa* in order to vindicate himself.

The clever man does not grasp at the burden of his previous knowledge but leaves it at the gates of the *hanaqa*, and for this reason the path for him is a current that leads to the ocean of Truth.

The stupid man tries to swim against the current and each hour grows weaker. To keep his body afloat and prolong for himself the pleasure of resistance, he reaches for every bush that grows on the bank and uses all his strength just to avoid being carried into the gloom of fear, emptiness, and oblivion.

Go and Study Yourself

One *shaikh* had only a few followers. People went to him unwillingly, for he created tests for those who wanted

54   That is, to the one who initiated him into Sufism (author's note).

to become his *murids*. One day two young men came to him and expressed the desire to become his disciples.

"What do you know?" asked the teacher.

"I speak three languages," answered one proudly. "I have mastered ancient philosophy, mathematics, and history."

"I too have studied scholarly things," said the second with sorrow, "but I don't know anything."

The Sufi let the second one stay but released the first.

"Why aren't you taking me?" asked the all-knowing man, surprised. "My companion even admitted he doesn't know anything."

"To the intelligent man," the Sufi answered, "earthly knowledge gives only the sensation that he knows nothing. Your learning is still too rudimentary to make even that clear to you. Go and study yourself."

On Avoiding Embarrassment to One's Shaikh

One must avoid at all costs placing the *shaikh* in a position where he might notice a transgression but, out of consideration, say nothing; such silence demonstrates that the *shaikh* considers the transgressing *murid* unworthy of even being corrected.

The messenger of Allah, may Allah bless and greet him, was endowed by Allah with the seal of particular delicacy; he considered anyone's words sacred and worthy of respect. Even once he had been accorded the Prophetic gift by Allah, he retained these qualities. On this subject a *hadith* passed down by Abu-Daud[55]:

Abdullah ibn Abu Hamzah,[56] peace to him, told how he had agreed with the Prophet, may Allah bless and greet him, concerning the sale of his things. This happened before the condescension of revelations to the Prophet from Allah. He had promised the Prophet, may Allah bless and greet him, to bring something to a certain place. But he happened to forget his promise. When he remembered it three days latter, Abdullah went to the place and was surprised to find there the Prophet, may Allah bless and greet him.

The Prophet said, "I was worried something might have happened to you. I've been waiting for you for three days."

---

55 Abu Daud (d. 889): author of *Kitab-Us-Sanan*, considered the fourth book of *sunna*.

56 Abu Hamzah: paternal uncle and foster brother of the Prophet Muhammad.

Part Two

The Murid and His Pir

On the Pir's Significance for the Murid

Sufi tradition maintains that the *murid* must believe that his *shaikh* is a veritable saint, a protégé of the Prophet Muhammad, may Allah bless and welcome him.

The *murid* is obliged to think of his *shaikh* as the most perfect man on earth. God guards his saints against the commission of sins, but they are living people and can sometimes allow errors that conceal within them certain idiosyncrasies. Having made such a mistake, the *shaikh* himself sees it immediately and then and there repents, and his repentance differs from that of simple mortals, such that the Most High, having acknowledged it, can raise him to a height that the simple man could not attain even through long years of service.

You must love your *shaikh*—so say the wise—with all your heart, and hope in him or in his ability to help you. His satisfaction with you is the satisfaction of the Most High, while the rejection of the *shaikh* is the rejection of the Most High.

✦ ✦ ✦

Do not feel bored, say the Sufis, if you do not experience some special states during *zikr* or other prayers to God. Mystical states can long escape the Sufi, and the reasons for this the *murid* must seek in himself.

Most often the absence of mystical revelations can be

linked to the lack of sincerity in one's service and to the
murid's desire to elicit such a state from God.

The alteration of state, they say, is not your goal. On the
contrary, you must guard against such things. And if some
sensations should be revealed to you, give thanks to the
Most High, for this means the discovery unto you of the
mercy of the Most High Allah.

◆ ◆ ◆

Yet more they say: be certain that if the *shaikh* should in
fact turn his attention to you, he can raise you to the level
attained by Djunaid,[57] mercy be upon him.

Only by the expression of humility, only by sincerely
loving your *shaikh*, may you hope to be vouchsafed at some
point with his favorable glance. For without such conviction there is no benefit whatsoever to you in this. The
slightest impediment will cut short the reception of *faiz*.[58]

Love for the *shaikh* should be pure and without ulterior
motive. It should be free of explanations of why it must
exist.

◆ ◆ ◆

A story is cited in the "Life of Amir Kulal" that demonstrates what the *murid*'s true attachment to his *shaikh*

---

57 Djunaid (also Junayd al-Baghdadi, d. 910): Sufi mystic originator
of subtle centers and cosmological correspondences in the body.
58 *Faiz* (also *fayd*): divine energy, effulgence.

should be like. [59] It is related that his holiness Amir Kulal, may mercy be upon him, once set out for the city of Nur. When he had approached the river and made his way across, he stopped for a short time. His holiness Amir Kulal was sunk in thought, and after some time he raised his head and said, "Friends, Ali Sufi has come!"

Now this Ali Sufi was one of his devoted servants, and he had been left at home in order to serve the brothers. Everyone was surprised because he had been left behind. Suddenly they see Ali Sufi walking like the wind along the surface of the water, and his feet are not wet. When he had crossed the river and approached his holiness, Amir Kulal scolded him, saying, "When did you leave home?"

Ali Sufi responded, "O *Hazrat*, my attraction to you took hold of me to such an extent that my will was no longer my own. Now I open my eyes and see myself in this place. My passion for you swallowed me up so much that I no longer knew myself."

His holiness Amir Kulal, may mercy be upon him, said, "In that case, as you've come, go back and be ready to serve when we return."

According to the *shaikh*'s orders, Ali Sufi again placed his feet on the surface of the water and set out on the road like the wind, immediately arriving at his place of service.

✦ ✦ ✦

59   Shikhab ad-din B. bint Amir Hamza, "The Life of Amir Kulal," in *Wisdom of the Sufis* (Russian). Saint Petersburg, 2001, pp. 51-52 (author's note).

They say that when Allah sees a soul that is conscientious and suffering for its sins, He hands it over to the Sufis for its lasting development. He has not yet come to love this hesitating soul, but He has turned His face towards it and placed hope in it with the passionate desire that, with the help of its *shaikh*, that soul should find the shortest path to Him. For this reason He brings the person to the *hanaqa* and puts him in the Sufis' hands.

And when the *murid* discovers, or rather, becomes suddenly aware of the importance with which Allah has treated him, he finally understands that he has been noticed, made the object of attention, and his heart grows joyful at the fact that he has begun, with the help of his *shaikh*, to fulfill his life's hidden meaning, even if it has not yet become altogether clear to him.

Thus is love for the *shaikh* born in the *murid's* heart, along with anxiety before the Perfect Human Being, the only person on earth to him, he who has traversed the path to God and knows how to lead his *murid* to Him.

♦ ♦ ♦

"No one finds his way without a mentor," says Mashrab,[60] may mercy be upon him.

They say that one day when Mashrab was on his way to his beloved *pir* Afaq Hodja,[61] he tied one end of a

---

60   Babarakhim Mashrab (d. 1711): Central Asian poet.
61   Afaq Hodja (d. 1693): Kashgari ruler.

rope around his neck and attached the other to the neck of the dog that accompanied him on his journeys. In this way he approached the door of the *hanaqa* and read a *mukhammas*[62] that contained the following lines:

> My faults without number,
> Sobbing, I come for forgiveness....
> To Thee I come, so that Thy mercy
> Should make whole my ailing soul....

◆ ◆ ◆

Each person who has made himself your slave, said Mashrab of his *shaikh*, has already attained salvation.

◆ ◆ ◆

Mashrab thus addressed his *shaikh* in verse: "You are the candle on the grave of the righteous, the oil of my lamp, the pupil of my eye."

◆ ◆ ◆

"My house is destroyed," continues Mashrab in a *ghazal*,[63] "no soul left in my body. I wander from courtyard to courtyard and, like an owl, have no nest. And as long as I do not see my *shaikh*, I shall have no roof above my head."

62 *Mukhammas*: genre of Persian poetry.
63 *Ghazal*: genre of Persian poetry.

♦ ♦ ♦

There are many legends about the second teacher of Mashrab, may mercy be upon him, the Kashgari saint Afaq Hodja, peace unto him, whose real name was Hodja Khidoyatulla. The nickname Afaq took hold during the time when people came from all around to become his *murids*. "Afaq" means vicinity, surroundings.

The *hazrat* had vast knowledge and not only in theology. In his youth he had studied the exact and theoretical sciences. And he knew Sufi poetry well.

The life history of Mashrab relates that in the seventeenth century the cities of Yarqend and Kashgar belonged to Abdullah Khan, whose habit it was to turn to his entourage for answers to difficult questions.[64]

Once when reading the poetry of Hafiz,[65] he happened upon two lines whose meaning he could not fathom. For some time he tried to unlock the puzzle of the poetry but then declared that he would become the *murid* of the man who could decipher the enigmatic lines.

None of the khan's courtiers or palace scholars was able to solve the mystery, but among the servants of the khan were several who frequented the *hanaqa* of Afaq Hodja.

64   *Divana-i-Mashrab.* Biography of the most popular representative of mysticism in the Turkmen region. Russian trans. by N. S. Lykoshin. Tashkent, 1992 (author's note).
65   Hafiz, also Hafez, of Shiraz (d. ca. 1388): Persian lyric poet of mystic Islam.

They spoke to the khan about their *shaikh*, and the khan ordered that Afaq Hodja be brought to the court in hopes that the holy man might explain to him the meaning of the lines imprinted in his mind.

Afaq Hodja was brought to the sovereign's court. Abdullah Khan greeted the Sufi with respect and asked him to take a place higher than all the other scholars and courtiers. Refreshments were served, and afterward the khan respectfully asked Afaq Hodja the meaning of the following Farsi lines:

> *Ta zimai-khona dami, nami nishan khogad-bud,*
> *Sarim mo khaki ragi Piri mugan khogad-bud.*

Afaq Hodja heard the verse and smiled in token of having understood the concealed meaning. First he pointed out a mistake that had crept into the couplet, namely the word *dami*, which should have been *mai* if the Arabic letter *dahal* had not been confused with the letter *waw*. The correction changed the meaning of the first line, such that in this redaction the lines could be translated thus:

> For as long as some sign or remnant remains
> Of the tavern or the wine (*mai*),
> May my head be dust along the tavern keeper's
>   path.

"By the word 'tavern,' Afaq Hodja explained, the earthly, transitory world should be understood. "The 'tavern keeper' is the Prophet Muhammad, may Allah bless and greet him. The wine is the word of Allah. As a whole the verses should be understood in this way: for as long as even the slightest trace or remnant of the divine word remains in the world, the believer's head should rest in the dust at the feet of the Prophet of the word of God.

"I myself am wandering in that world," continued Afaq Hodja sadly, "with the sole hope that I might be favored with the attention of the Prophet, may Allah bless and greet him."

Abdullah Khan was elated and respectfully took the hand of the saint, kissing it and passing it before his eyes to show that from that moment he would enter among the *murids* of Afaq Hodja. All the scholars and courtiers followed the example of their sovereign and became *murids* of the holy man, may mercy be upon him. [66]

It is related in the life history of Mashrab that among the followers of the Naqshbandi Order, Afaq Hodja attained the highest stages and instructed all his devoted *murids*.

Every day in the *hanaqa* of the saint, like moths flocking to the light, his numerous *murids* would gather into a circle for performing their rites. They would throw themselves down where their *pir* had walked, their eyes glued to his hands. Some drowned themselves in self-renunciation and shed abundant tears.

They say that Afaq Hodja would satisfy himself daily with but three swallows of food. In his talks, he explained to his *murids* the content of the book of Masnavi-

---

66 *Divana-i-Mashrab*, pp. 10-12 (author's note).

Sharif,[67] accompanying his explanations with profound instruction.

Afaq Hodja was equally gracious toward the poor, the destitute, and the mentally disturbed, all of whom he attempted to calm and console, causing distress to none.

During his life, Afaq Hodja devoted much time and energy to constructing magnificent mosques and buildings for the rites of the dervishes. In 1693 Afaq Hodja fell ill and died in Yarqend. The holy man's tomb in Kashgar serves as a place for the pious worship of pilgrims.

---

67 *Masnavi-Sharif* (The Poem of Hidden Meaning) of Jalaluddin Rumi (author's note).

On the Pir's Knowledge

The *murid* must believe that the *pir* knows all the slightest circumstances of his life.

It is stated in the Qur'an:

> Verily, if Allah willed it, He could have sealed your heart, and erased the falsehood and affirmed the truth with His words. He is fully aware of your innermost thoughts. [68]

It sometimes seems to me that my movement along the path is like digging a well with a thimble. It is indeed that, for the mountains of spiritual filth that have clung to the heart through years of thoughtless and irresponsible, sinful life are impossible to clear away in a day. It is the task of Sisyphus, comparable to carrying a stone to the top of a hill, from which it rolls back if the body and soul do not stop sinning. It is akin to growing a delicate flower in the white-hot sand of the desert. If the *shaikh* does not indicate the road, the stone rolls back down, the flower wilts.

There is discord and confusion in my soul. As always the *hazrat* comes to my aid, barely seeing me where I sit in the distance but feeling and knowing everything about me. I am convinced of this. For as soon as my soul grows

68   Qur'an 42:24.

disturbed, before it has had time even to make sense of the disturbance and form questions, an answer to them appears during our regular conversation, and I am surprised to hear suddenly from the *hazrat*:

"When has the devil let us serve God without impediments? He does everything in his power to divert us from the righteous path and invents hundreds of different tricks depending upon where he finds our weakness. If you happen to doubt in your abilities or the path comes to seem too difficult, that is where the devil appears in order to whisper in your ear: 'drop it why don't you; you're not up to this road.'"

"He's talking about me," I think and immediately am rapt with attention. My glance happens to fall on the young *murids* seated around me, and I see by their faces that they are thinking the same.

Shaikh Ibrahim continues:

> Most often the devil watches for moments of inattention. He urges us to commit improper acts, suggests sinful ideas and impermissible foods, and he proposes joining in dubious activities. And if he can't catch us in our human weaknesses, he begins to work on our merits.

"That's all about me," I continue to think, sinking still lower. "Every word is about me and my weaknesses. I thought about that myself today. The *murid* was right when he warned me that it wasn't always necessary to formulate a question and rush up to the skaikh with it. It's enough that the question appear in your heart. You'll hear an answer to it from the *shaikh.*"

"For example," continues the *hazrat,* "every night one *murid* conscientiously performs a fixed quantity of prayers of the name of God during his *zikr.* Then it seems to him that it won't cost him anything to double the quantity of prayers and he does so and begins to be proud. That's it. It's enough for the devil. He has caught the man through the weakness of vainglory.

♦ ♦ ♦

The words of Abu Sulaiman ad-Darani[69] come to mind: "Everything that distracts you from Allah is your misfortune." I immediately want to share my knowledge with others but stop myself in time. "Oh, my Lord!" I think. "How much more must I work in order to bring such self-importance and vainglory to naught? It is true after all that everything that distracts me from Allah is my misfortune."

I recall hearing in the *hanaqa* that the Sufi concerns himself with what pacifies his disposition. And then, through the mercy of the Most High, traits of humility appear in all his physical and spiritual aspect. But all it takes is for him to think that he is indeed producing the impression of a humble and righteous man on others for the devil to appear beside him.

"Oh, you hypocrite!" begins the devil, attacking the hesitant man. "You are only pretending to be humble. What

---

69 Abu Sulaiman ad-Darani (d. 820): source of *ahadith.*

motivates you isn't righteousness; it's your insatiable vainglory."

The man is shamed. At which point another danger appears: from one extreme he may swing to the other. He begins to reprove himself and his vainglory. His self-reproof and self-flagellation can proceed to such a point that he might again open the door to the devil's trickery and step onto the easy path of exaggerating his own personal weakness and blame, which can then grow into a kind of ecstasy over his own worthlessness.

"Oh, you hypocrite!" jumps in the devil once more. "You think you can trick me? You cannot! I see you taking secret pleasure in your own worthlessness and weaknesses. Your vainglory is merely continuing to hide behind the guise of a man who's reproaching himself. . . ."

◆ ◆ ◆

Once in my distant youth I was caught in a sand storm in the steppe. The wind twisted the sand into plaits, lifting it above the tops of the dunes, then dropping it into the valleys.

The wind carried the sand, torn baby's breath, and dried weeds through the steppe. It rushed violently up and down, hung above the earth, then unexpectedly whirled around my feet.

I threw myself into a small declivity and lay there for several hours, deafened by the wind's explosions, blinded by the streams of dust, and nearly carried off completely by the sand.

My doubts and hesitations of today, my casting to and fro, is none other than a dust storm that blinds and deafens me to the main thing: a frightening and inextinguishable passion that envelopes my soul with emptiness.

I open the Qur'an and tears immediately fill my eyes, for I read:

> *Have you not noticed the one whose god is his passion? And Allah has sent him astray despite his knowledge, sealed his hearing and his heart, and placed a veil before his eyes.*[70]

✦ ✦ ✦

I often used to wonder why I feel ashamed in the first few moments of being in the *hanaqa*, seated next to my *shaikh*. And then I understood: once inside the *hanaqa*, in giving myself up to the will of a Perfect Person, I myself become meek without effort, a person without a shadow of pretense or hypocrisy, for here the need to show off the peacock's feathers that conceal one's vainglory falls away.

In the *hanaqa* my vanity becomes like a frightened little puppy, fearful in the face of danger, its tail between its legs.

My ruminations are cut short by the voice of our *shaikh*, who, after a long silence, pronounces:

70   Qur'an 45:23.

Forget that you are Sufis. Perform your duties conscientiously and remember God. When a *murid* begins to think that he is traveling along the difficult path of perfecting his soul, he inevitably leaves the devil an opportunity to take hold of his pride and self-pity. Indeed you are Sufis. But only so long as you yourselves do not remember it.

♦ ♦ ♦

Shaikh Muhammad Zahid,[71] may mercy be upon him, was one of the beloved and devoted pupils of the great Shaikh Ubaydullah Ahrar Vali, may his grave be sacred. It was precisely to this pupil that, after the death of Hodja Ahrar, according to spiritual priority, the secret blessing of the Naqshbandi Order's honorable line passed.

They say that Shaikh Zahid, may mercy be upon him, was a paragon of godliness, purity, and asceticism. He was the devoted *murid* and caretaker of the secrets of Shaikh Ubaydullah Ahrar. Shaikh Zahid composed a book of worthy and laudable qualities of his *shaikh* and named it *Silsilatul'-arifin va tazkiratu as-siddikin*, or *A Chain of Holy Names and Remembrance of Righteous Men*.

In it the following is written:

"I had the honor of serving under Shaikh Ubaydullah Ahrar for twelve years, thanks be to Allah! I became acquainted with the *shaikh* under the following circumstances. I had left my home with another man by the name of

71 Shaikh Muhammad as-Zahid Vali

Shaikh Nigmatulla from Samarqand in search of knowledge. We set out for Herat. When we reached the village of Shadman, we stopped for several days because of the severe heat. During our stay there, we learned that Shaikh Ubaydullah Ahrar, may mercy be upon him, had arrived in the village. We went to visit him, and he asked me, 'Where are you from?'"

"'Samarqand,' I answered.

"He began a most interesting conversation with us, during which he began little by little to uncover what I concealed from him, even informing me of my reason for traveling to Herat. He knew everything about me. When I learned this, my heart was drawn to him.

"Then he said, 'If your desire is to acquire knowledge, that is attainable even here,' at which I became utterly convinced that not a single one of my thoughts was unknown to him. Still, the yearning to travel to Herat was not loosed from my heart. But just then our conversation was interrupted, and the *shaikh* left us.

"I was extremely anxious to see him again, but one of his followers informed us that the *shaikh* was occupied in writing something. I waited, and when he was free, he came to me and said, 'Tell me honestly, is your desire to study in Herat dictated by a yearning to receive the usual religious training or do you want to attain the Sufi *tariqat*?'

"I was astounded at the depth of his knowledge and listened to each of his words with utmost care. My companion answered him: 'The desire to receive the Sufi *tariqat* has overwhelmed him. He only pretends to be searching for the usual training.'

"The *shaikh* smiled and said, 'If that is so, such yearning is praiseworthy.'

"Then he led me toward his garden. We walked until no one else could see us anymore. Then he stopped, and from the moment he took my hand, I fell into complete forgetfulness for a long time. When I came to myself, he again began to speak with me, may Allah be pleased with him.

"And he said, 'You are probably capable of reading my epistle," upon which he pulled from his pocket a small piece of paper, read it through, lowered it, and spread it before me, saying, 'Learn what is written here, and if the writing contains the truth of prayer, then humility, godliness, and submission will arise in your heart from the contemplation of Allah's greatness. Such happiness depends upon the presence of love for the Most High God, and love in turn is founded upon the observance of the living path and works of the Prophet Muhammad, may Allah bless him and greet him with the best and most perfect blessings and greetings. And the correct observance of the Prophet Allah depends upon true knowledge of his teachings. Therefore, may his teachings be with the people, may you study among them, for they are the heirs and preservers of religious knowledge! Receive from them the healthful learning until you should be honored with divine mercy. . . .'

"Then he returned to the *hanaqa*, read the *surah* 'Al-Fatiha and bid me to continue on to Herat.

"I set out, as he instructed me, for Bukhara. I had not proceeded even a few steps when he sent after me a book for Shaikh Kalan-Hazrat, a descendant of the great imam and maulana Sagduddin al'-Kashgari,[72] may their graves be sacred, in which the following inscription had been made: 'To you falls the obligation of observing and looking after the mystical states of the carrier of this book and preserving him from the cares of the world.'

"Seeing the way he treated me, all my heart was gripped by love and devotion. But I remained stubborn in my intension. I took the book and set off on my way. But I could not proceed fast enough. After only two or three posting stations, my horse was so exhausted that it could not continue. In the end, I changed six horses before arriving in Bukhara.

"I had barely arrived when my eyes were stricken with illness. Several days later, once my health had returned, I was preparing to continue my journey when I came down with a fever. It occurred to me that if I set out in that condition, I could die on the road. And I relinquished my former intention, set aside the hope of continuing my journey, and decided to return to the service of Shaikh Ubaydullah Ahrar, my Allah be pleased with him!

"When I arrived in Tashkent, I first wanted to visit Shaikh Ilias Gishka. I left my clothes, books, and horse with a friend and set out to see him. Along the way I met one of the servants of Shaikh Ilias and said, 'Let us go to visit the *shaikh*.'

"'Where is your horse?' he asked.

"I answered that I had left it with another man, and he said, 'Bring him to my yard. Then we'll visit the *shaikh*.'

---

72 Sagduddin al'-Kashgari (also Sa'd al-Din Kashgari, d. 1456).

"When I returned for my horse, I heard a voice that said, 'Your horse and all your things are lost.'

"I was completely taken aback and had no idea what to do. I sat down to consider what had happened, and the thought sprung from my heart that this might very well have occurred because of the displeasure of Ubaydullah Ahrar with my desire to visit Shaikh Ilias, for Sufi *shaikhs* are jealous of their followers.

"'Why should Hazrat Ubaydullah, may Allah be pleased with him, be devoted to you with all his being if you intend to visit some other *shaikh*?! Therefore do you deserve to be punished and even more.'

"And I turned from my intention to visit Shaikh Ilias and decided first of all to visit our Shaikh Ubaydullah Ahrar.

"I had hardly finished formulating such a thought when a man came to me to say that my horse and my things had been found. I went to the friend who had kept my things for me, and he said, 'Oh, Muhammad! I had barely tied up your horse when it disappeared from sight. I looked for it everywhere without finding it, and I began to despair. Then I came back and found it standing in the middle of the marketplace amid the people. Not a single item from the baggage on it had disappeared, despite the crowd's commotion.

"I was astounded at his words, and I took the horse and set out for Samarqand. When I came to Shaikh Ubaydullah, may mercy be upon him, he smiled upon me and said, 'Welcome!'"

"And I never ventured beyond his threshold again."

◆ ◆ ◆

I recall the words of Shaikh Abdudallah Ansari,[73] may mercy be upon him. Hazrat Ansari said that there are three things the *murid* can never change about himself, but that his *shaikh* concerns himself with:

- ◆ Desiring before thinking
- ◆ Desiring more than thinking
- ◆ Desiring what belongs to others.

This is indeed the case: I had proceeded along the path only a few paces before managing to commit an implausible number of mistakes, correcting which was impossible without the help of my *shaikh*. Only then did I understand with all my heart why the wise maintained that it was impossible to traverse the path without the help of a mentor.

And now I am ashamed at my haste: the beads of sweat had hardly formed on my forehead when I began secretly awaiting the mercy of the Most High and impatiently wondering why my efforts had not been noted. I must still await my allotted fate, and here I am already expecting rewards.

And wasn't it I who looked with envious eyes upon those *murids* whose faces had already begun to shine with light, while they were so humble that they even seemed ashamed at the beauty that God had begun to note in them? Indeed I too want to obtain such mercy. And again shame at

73   Abdullah Ansari: Companion of the Prophet Muhammad.

myself rises up from the depths of my heart, and my face turns a deep shade, while unanticipated tears fill my eyes.

+ + +

Hazrat Mashrab, may mercy be upon him, said:

> Without becoming a moth, it's impossible to burn
>   in the candle.
> If there are no pearls, there's no need for mother-
>   of-pearl.

One can clean the outside, but if the human heart is caked in the filth of unrighteous deeds and, like a neglected swamp, is covered with thick slime, then such a heart is suffocating without divine light, slowly sinking into darkness.

The moth forgets about itself as it yearns for the light, knowing no fear and feeling no heat from the bright light of the lamp. It strives toward the light, singing its wings, but continues to strive with all its being.

Mashrab, may mercy be upon him, said:

> The beloved does not want your heart
> If there are no wounds in it.

Only unrequited yearning for God—Sufis maintain—can burn down the veil that separates man from God, in the fire of love.

Mashrab, may his grave by sacred, has also said:

A moth having turned its face toward the desert of
   love—
My heart....
A tear hanging like a drop of rain
From my glistening eyelash....

Recounted in the life history of Mashrab, may mercy
be upon him, is an episode describing his service to his *pir*
Afaq Hodja.

"O, Sufis!" Afaq Hodja once addressed his *murids*, "do
you know that a holy fool has come to us from the region
of Islam and that he is crying at the door to the *hanaqa*?
Bring the poor man here."

Two *murids* went out and found a young man with a
beard just beginning to grow, a full, beautiful face, and
large fiery eyes beneath thick brows.

They had never before seen such a dervish. The
murids brought the holy fool to their teacher. Afaq Hodja
asked that he be brought closer. The two *murids* picked
up Mashrab under the arms and placed him at the feet of
their teacher. The *shaikh* took Mashrab by the hand and
asked, "Where have you come from, holy fool?"

"Bukhara," answered Mashrab.

"Well, they say that even the donkeys in Bukhara have
tongues," joked the teacher, once he had heard Mashrab
recite his *ghazals*. Then he looked graciously on his guest,
spread his hands before him, and pronounced a prayer for
Mashrab's desires to be fulfilled, gently patting him on the
shoulder.

Mashrab fell into a faint like a wounded bird, and Afaq Hodja took his head and placed it on his lap. The *ishan*[74] cast his penetrating gaze upon the soul of Mashrab and saw that the lamp within was filled with oil and the wick was prepared but that the poor man had been constrained to wander, not having found a mentor capable of lighting it.

Turning to his *murids* who had gathered around him, Afaq Hodja said, "Be witnesses: I shall give the name Mashrab to this holy fool."[75]

"*Allahu Aqbar!*" (God is great), shouted his *murids* in one voice.

Mashrab came to himself and recited a new *ghazal*. He looked upon the state of his soul and understood that it no longer resembled its former self and that by comparison with the secret forms of knowledge, those commonly known among the people were like crafts to true art.

Afaq Hodja said to him graciously, "O, Mashrab. Stay with me to serve."

Mashrab stood and bowed to the teacher.

For three years Mashrab carried firewood. For another three he carried water in wineskins. For another he lay on the threshold of the *ishan*'s dwelling. Over the course of these seven years he wore only a short coat, in summer with its fur turned out, in winter with it turned in.[76]

---

74 *Ishan* (Persian, "they"): employed in Central Asia as a term for teacher, instructor.

75 His actual name was Boborahim. Mashrab means "the way that leads to God" as well as "tavern," a connection that underlines the quality of being drunk with God (author's note).

76 *Divana-i-Mashrab*, pp. 57-60 (author's note).

On Proper Posture

In the presence of the *shaikh*, during gatherings, one must sit properly, without the need even for changing one's position. When water sits peacefully in a glass, every representation is clearly visible in it; if the water is disturbed, then no object is clearly reflected in its surface.

Beside one's *shaikh*—said Sufis of old—one must sit as if in prayer, so still that a bird, taking one for an inanimate object, might land on one's head. According to tradition, so sat beside the Prophet Muhammad, may Allah bless and greet him, his comrades, may mercy be upon them.

The following *hadith* is cited by at-Tabrani on this account.

"Usama ibn Shereeq said:

"'In the presence of the Messenger of Allah, may Allah bless and greet him, we sat so still that it was as if we feared startling birds on our heads. No one dared to open his mouth.

"'After some moments, several men approached and asked, 'Who is the most dear to God among His servants?'

"'The Prophet responded, 'He who has the most moral character.'"

On Obtaining Permission

In beginning something, it is essential mentally to obtain the permission and help of one's *shaikh*. Hazrat Ahrar says that whether the *pir* is present in the flesh or not, the thoughts of the *murid* always lie between the *pir's* brows and will always be known to him.

Even if your *shaikh* is far away—so Sufis say—you must behave as if he is right beside you. Anything even the least bit connected to the *shaikh's* name must be done with him in mind. The man who does not fear the wrath of his *shaikh* does not fear the wrath of Allah.

Sufis maintain that the *murid* who doubts the holiness and strength of his *shaikh* will never attain happiness. History contains no shortage of testimonials to the fact that when young *murids* have, through excessive self-confidence, doubted in the abilities of their *shaikh*, God has turned away from them as from apostates.

Ibn Hajar al'-Haitami,[77] may his grave be sacred, tells a story he heard from Abu Sa'id Abdullah ibn Abi 'Asrun.[78] He in turn recounted a tale in which he himself took part:

"I came to Baghdad in search of knowledge and began to accompany ibn Saqa to his studies in the Nizamiya medresse. We also went to visit righteous Sufis. Shaikh

---

77   Ibn Hajar al-Haitami (d. 1567).
78   Abu Sa'id Abdullah ibn Abi'Asrun (d. 1189): Islamic theologian.

Yusuf Hamadani, may mercy be upon him, also lived in Baghdad at the time.

"We decided to visit him and set out in a party of three: ibn Saqa, Shaikh Abdulqadir, then a young man,[79] and I. On the way to Shaikh Yusuf Hamadani, may mercy be upon him, ibn Saqa said, 'I plan to ask the *shaikh* a question to which he will have no answer.'

"I said, 'I'll ask him a question and see what his answer is.'

"Shaikh Abdulqadir said, 'God forbid I should ask him anything! I shall place myself before him and await a blessing through his glance alone!'

"We were able to see him only an hour after hour our arrival. Shaikh Hamadani looked with anger upon ibn Saqa and said, 'Woe unto you, ibn Saqa! You want to ask me a question to which I have no answer? Your question is such and the answer is such. I see the flame of unbelief (*qufr*) burns within you.'

"Then he turned to me and said, 'O, Abdullah! You want to ask me a question and see what I respond? Your question is such and the answer to it is such. Let peace come to your ears for your absence of tact and decorum!'

"Then he turned to Shaikh Abdulqadir, approached him, and warmly greeted him, saying, 'O, Abdulqadir! You are honored with the pleasure of Allah and his Messenger Muhammad thanks to the beauty of your upbringing and courtesy. I see you as if pronouncing sermons in Baghdad,

---

79   Abdulqadir (d. 1166): future founder of the Qadiriya Sufi brotherhood.

seated before the people, rich and poor alike. And you say: 'My foot lies upon the neck of each *vali*. [80] And I see how the Sufis of your time have lowered their necks out of respect for you.'

"Afterward Shaikh Hamadani left us, and we saw him no more.

"As for Abdulqadir, signs appeared that testified to his nearness to Allah. Simple mortals and chosen ones began to flock to him. And once, at the zenith of his fame, he pronounced the words, 'My foot lies upon the neck of each *vali*!' And all the holy men of that time recognized the truth of this.

"As for ibn Saqa, he studied the *shari'at*, or Muslim religious law, and became an expert, surpassing many of the learned men of his time. He was renowned for being able to defeat anyone with whom he debated religious learning. He was eloquent and of striking appearance. The Caliph brought him near and later sent him as an emissary to the Byzantine Emperor.

"The Emperor was surprised and delighted with him, recognizing his expertise in science and rhetoric, and seeing him as a man of impeccable behavior. Religious leaders and scholars from among the Christians gathered around ibn Saqa. He engaged them in discussions and silenced them with his arguments. They were unable to out debate him, and his learned fame grew in the eyes of the Emperor and elsewhere.

80   *vali* (also *wali*): title used for person whom God has taken into His proximity and who is fulfilling the proper end of human existence.

"He was shown the Emperor's daughter, who pleased him. He was enraptured with her and asked her father for her hand in marriage. She said she would agree to become his wife only if he became a Christian. He did so and married her. Then he grew ill, and they tossed him out on the market square, where he became a beggar, asking for bread and finding no sympathy among the people.

"Somehow a Muslim he knew saw him and asked, 'What has happened to you?'

"Ibn Saqa responded, 'Temptation seduced me and transformed me into what you see.'

"The other asked, 'Do you remember anything at all from the Qur'an?'

"Ibn Saqa responded, 'Nothing but the words of Allah:

> Perhaps those who disbelieve will wish they were Muslims. [81]

Then he said, "I gave him alms, after which I saw him anew. He was all in a fire and at his last gasp. I turned him in the direction of *qibla*, toward Mecca, and he turned toward the East, in the direction of Baghdad. I turned him toward Mecca, and he again turned to the East. And thus until the moment he let free his spirit. His face was turned toward the East, he repeated the words of Yusuf Hamadani, and knew that he had be punished by reason of the *shaikh*'s words.

"And Shaikh Abu Sa'id Abdullah ibn Abi'Asrun said, 'As for myself, I returned to Damascus, where the righteous

---

[81] Qur'an 15:2.

Sultan as-Shahid[82] drew me to his person and engaged me as the manager of his *vaqf*.[83] I took on this responsibility and became immersed in secular affairs. All the words of Shaikh Hamadani pronounced before us came true.

And indeed the Qur'an states:

> *Whosoever performs good does so for his own soul;*
> *whosoever performs evil does so against it.*[84]

✦ ✦ ✦

Mystical education presupposes a lengthy sojourn with God on the part of the *murid*'s heart. The *murid* resembles a pearl diver whose only thought is obtaining the jewel from the bottom of the sea. Having taken a chest-ful of air, he plunges into the depth that ordinary people do not attempt without a mask. When he arrives at the *hanaqa*, like the diver, the *murid* distances himself from the world, plunging into conversation with his *shaikh*, attempting to take hold of the profound meaning of every word, every hint.

✦ ✦ ✦

82 Sultan ash-Shahid (also Sultan as-Salih Ayyub) of Damascus (d. 1249).

83 *Vaqf* (also *waqf*): religious endowments; property in Muslim countries withheld from the state on the basis of religious or charitable use.

84 Qur'an 45:15.

It was said by the teachers of the Hodjagon Tariqat, may the mercy of Allah be upon them:

> Receive the *tavajuh*[85] in the hearts of the *shaikhs* (the men of the *tariqat*) with fullness and peace, for this creates a place for your *nafs* in the hearts of the *shaikhs* (the men of the *tariqat*). They are, after all, the *shaikhs* of the *tariqat*! The breath must be conserved exactly in the manner of the *tariqat shaikhs*, may the mercy of Allah be upon them. Nothing must issue from you that might serve as a reason for the disproof of the *shaikhs'* thoughts. In order to reach this level, all your desires must be the desires of the *shaikhs*, while the desires of the *shaikhs* must be your desires. A man thereby is ennobled and attains happiness.

✦ ✦ ✦

In instructing their *murids*, the *shaikhs* of the Naqshbandi Order used in past times to practice a certain discipline that, like the *rabita*,[86] presupposes the linkage between the *murid's* heart and that of his teacher. Today

85 *Tavajuh*: practice of the pupil who concentrates on the mental image of his *shaikh*, which creates a point of spiritual contact between him and his teacher, and then a spiritual union between them (author's note).
86 *Rabita*: isolated shelter; small, secluded monastery; psychological practice of the Sufis: a spiritual link to the mentor by means of the creation of his image in the heart of his pupil; the dissolution of the pupil's self in that image (author's note).

the essence of this discipline remains as before: the *murid* is faced with the task of representing to himself the image of his *shaikh* as often as possible, particularly when the *shaikh* is not physically present beside him.

In such a manner, a constant connection is maintained between *murids* and their *shaikhs*, while an unbroken stream of divine knowledge and energy flows into the heart of the seeker.

✦ ✦ ✦

They say that during the time of Hodja Ahrar, may mercy be upon him, an act of initiation into the *rabita* would take place. The story is told of when Hodja Ahrar, peace unto him, exhorted his son Muhammad Yakhia to follow the path of the *rabita* .... The boy asked whether he should look his father in the eye or upon his face, and the *hazrat* placed his index finger between his brows, upon which his son understood where to direct his gaze. [87]

Today too this principle of the *rabita* is observed in the Naqshbandi Order. The *murid* plants within himself the image of his *shaikh*, imagining him in different parts of his body, and then plunging the image into his heart. As the result of long training, the *murid* is able to call up the image of his teacher at any moment when his *shaikh*'s assistance becomes necessary. The constant presence of the *shaikh* in the *murid*'s heart is thought to help him avoid

---

87 *Sufism in Central Asia: Collected Essays in Memory of Fritz Maier* (Russian). Saint Petersburg, 2001, p. 101 (author's note).

straying from the path and to be especially useful in the battle with his own *nafs*, as well as in the struggle with the extraneous and alien intentions that tend to weaken the effectiveness of the seeker's prayerful repetition of God's name during the *zikr*.

On Avoiding Evil

One must not enter into close relations with people who do not believe in one's *shaikh*, nor visit their gatherings.

The *shari'at* condemns scandalous backbiting. Unequivocal proof of this is found in the Qur'an.

Allah says:

Nor shall you backbite one another. [88]

And elsewhere God says:

Woe to every backbiter, slanderer. [89]

✦ ✦ ✦

Abu Huraira, [90] may mercy be upon him, let it be known that the Messenger of Allah, may Allah bless and greet him, once asked his followers, 'Do you know what backbiting is?"

They responded, "Allah and his Messenger know better."

"Your reference to something concerning your brother, in his absence, that it would be unpleasant for him to hear."

---

88   Qur'an 49:12
89   Qur'an 104:1
90   Abu Huraira: Companion of the Prophet Muhammad, source of *ahadith*.

+ + +

The ulema say that it is the obligation of each person who overhears a piece of malicious gossip about a Muslim to confront and prevent the slanderer from continuing. If he cannot impede him with words, then he must stop him with his hand. If neither of these is effective, then he must rise up and leave the gathering. And if he hears that some are slandering his *shaikh*, then his care in performing the above should be that much greater.

+ + +

Abu Ad-Dara,[91] may Allah be pleased with him, recounted that the Messenger of Allah, may Allah bless and greet him, said, 'Allah will turn the face of the man who has deterred an insult to the honor of his brother away from the fire on Judgment Day.'[92]

+ + +

Mu'az ibn Anas,[93] may mercy be upon him, recounted that the Prophet, the peace and blessing of Allah unto him, said:

91   Abu Ad-Dara (also al-Daraqutni, ad-Daraqutni): scholar and source of *ahadith*.
92   Cited by at-Tirmidhi (author's note).
93   Mu'az ibn Anas (also Mu'adh ibn Anas al-Juhani): source of *ahadith*.

He who defends a believer from a hypocrite will
be sent by Allah an angel to protect him even from
the fire of Judgment Day. And he who accuses a
Muslim of something with the aim of dishonoring
him Allah will suspend from a bridge in hell until
he recants. [94]

❖ ❖ ❖

They say that once his Holiness Amir Kulal, may mercy
be upon him, set out for the assembly mosque of Bukhara
in the company of his supporters. A man was working
with one of his servants on a floor, and the servant asked
him, "Who are those people?"

The master responded, "Consumers of gifts."

When the man said this to his servant, Amir Kulal, may
mercy be upon him, said, "O my friends, his holiness and
our master Hodja Abdulhaliq Gizhduvani, may Allah be-
stow mercy upon him, deigned to say:

Every man who looks upon dervishes with disdain
will not depart from this world without being covered with scabs.

His brothers were surprised to hear such a pronouncement from his Holiness, but his *murids* did not know of
this event. And when on returning from the assembly

94   Cited by at-Tirmidhi (author's note).

mosque they approached that spot, they saw that the man had been consumed by an inner fire such that he had no peace or relief. And when his glance fell upon Amir Kulal, he understood from which bow the arrow had flown. And he said, "Take me to Amir Kulal, since what I said was uncalled for."

And when he had been brought to Amir Kulal, his Holiness said, "An arrow from the bow has fallen on this man. His illness cannot be healed. Take him back home."

And he had not yet reached his home before he departed this world.[95]

＋ ＋ ＋

One of the most characteristic traits of the Sufi is the fact that he pays no attention to insults intended for him. Our *hazrat* even says that it is better when a Sufi is insulted and humiliated. In such circumstances a person learns to develop humility and submission. But the main thing is that he should learn to be patient and suffer in the name of his Lord.

Abdullah Dihlawi tells of how Shaikh Abu Tahir[96] was once walking across the marketplace when someone hurled the mocking accusation, "*Ei, pir zindiki,*" which means, "Hey, teacher of the faithless." A *murid* of the *shaikh* who was beside him then, having heard the insult directed at his teacher, grew terribly angry and burned with the

95 *Wisdom of the Sufis,* pp. 90-91 (author's note).
96 Shaikh Abu Tahir: eighteenth-century scholar of *ahadith.*

desire to take the offender to account. But his *shaikh* calmly stopped him, saying, "Have patience."

In order to soothe the ire of his *murid*, when they had arrived home the *pir* showed him a sheaf of letters in which the authors—who were the leading officials of the country—appealed to him with the utmost respect, courtesy, and admiration, employing the very highest of titles.

"Each person," said the *shaikh* to his *murid*, "has his own opinion or understanding of me, according to the limits of his knowledge and the position he occupies in society. All opinion or understanding is but the expression of the wisdom, abilities, and position of a person. If someone calls me a *zindik*, why should we start a quarrel because of the reflection of his own ignorance? It is clear that such a reflection does not represent my true person or all that accords with it. We mustn't live under the influence of such irresponsible behavior. Even if it is insulting to us, God alone has the right and the power to punish the offender. We do not. Who are we to take the law of Allah into our own hands and exact vengeance?"

+ + +

The teacher of our *tariqat*, Hazrat Abdulkhaliq Gizhduvani, instructed his followers that the Sufi must not give in to personal insult, must not be offended by ill deeds or evil people: all his thoughts, every inward and every outward breath, must be directed toward the attainment of eternal blessedness. On which the following *rubai*:

My friends, in this world we are guests.
Keep no insults in your heart. Cease
Thinking of revenge, for he who is evil to another
In this life has enough malice as it is. [97]

◆ ◆ ◆

Another of the teachers of our *tariqat*, Hazrat Ali Romitani, [98] was asked, "What is faith?"

"Removal and attachment," answered the *hazrat*. "What precisely is removed and to what attached is the symbol of your faith. Remove your heart from the world. Attach it to God." [99]

The representatives of the school of Hodjagon, may the mercy of Allah be upon them, called their order *Marandj i marandjon*, which means "Offend no one and take no offense." "For as long as we remain adherents of this school and wear our Sufi garments," they said, "we shall take no offense if someone should cause us insult, and by turn, we shall offend no one."

◆ ◆ ◆

Hazrat Ali Hujviri, [100] may mercy be upon him, offers us a story of how insult can be accepted with gratitude

97   *Rubai* (pl. *rubaiyat*): Sufi verse form.
98   Hazrat Ali Romitani (d. 1316): *shaikh* of the Hodjagon Order
99   Abdurrahman Jami. *Evening Garden* (Russian). Dushanbe, 1964, p. 35 (author's note).
100   Shaikh Ali al-Hujviri (d. ca. 1073).

by the enamored friends of God, when he states, "Insult or hatred of Sufi holy men is actually a refreshing garden for them." Then he recounts the following story of Hazrat Ibrahim Adham, [101] peace unto him.

A man once asked Hazrat Ibrahim Adham whether he had ever satisfied the deepest desire of his heart during his long Sufi life.

The Sufi responded, "Yes, at least twice. Once I was traveling by boat. My clothes were tattered and filthy, my hair disheveled. The people did not know who I was, so seeing me in such a ragged state, my fellow travelers insulted me, pulled my hair, and made me the true laughing-stock of the voyage.

"That was the first time when the most prized desire of my heart was fulfilled and the cup of my happiness overflowed. But it was short-lived, for on the next day one man approached and literally urinated on my clothing, which, according to the law of the *shari'at*, I was then obliged to change.

"When I did so, the people grew more careful and ceased to make fun of me, and I lost my happiness.

"The second occasion of the fulfillment of my heart's most cherished wish took place on a rainy day in the bleak of winter. I was traveling and wet to the bone. I was searching for shelter, and when I came to the nearest village the rain was streaming from my *djubba* robe.

"I sought shelter in the mosque, but was not allowed

---

101   Hazrat Ibrahim Adham (also Abu Ishaq Ibrahim Adham): ninth century Sufi of Khorasan.

in and, in truth, was sorely ill-treated there. It was cold and, in order to warm up somehow, I made my way into the bath furnace and sat, being careful to keep my clothing from the flames. The smoke and suit of the fire turned my face and clothes black, so that when I came out, I was unrecognizable.

"That, my friend, was the second time the most cherished desire of my heart was fulfilled. I was extraordinarily happy with this ordeal, sent to me from my beloved God."

♦ ♦ ♦

The incomparable Naqshband Sufi Hodja Amir Kulal, may mercy be upon him, said that for the man who demonstrates submission before Allah, the Most High will raise his station. In the "Life of Amir Kulal" the following history is recounted.

They say that on one occasion, his Holiness Amir Kulal set out on a pilgrimage with several of his followers to the divinely lit shrine of his Holiness Hodja Muhammad Bobo. When they had covered a portion of the way, it happened that a lion had come into that steppe and was standing on the road without giving way.

The supporters took fright, and when his Holiness Amir Kulal approached, he saw what had happened and immediately went to the lion, took it by the neck, and led it to the side of the road, where he left it.

The supporters passed, seeing that the lion had lowered its head to the ground, as a man does in token of respect.

When they had taken this in, the supporters asked his Holiness the Amir, "O, *Hazrat*, what is it we have just seen?"

His Holiness Amir Kulal said, "Know, my friends, and be aware, that to each of us who displays fear before the Lord Most High and Benificent, both in his external manifestations and in the depths of his soul, the Great and Glorious Lord will cause all things to fear him...."

And then he said, "The Creator, may His name be extolled, made nothing master over man, such that he should fear it; rather every other thing will fear man on condition that he in turn fears God, the great and glorious. One must constantly fear the Lord Most High, and refrain from giving offense to anything at all, such that, as a result, salvation and the highest states of perfection will be accessible to you."[102]

There was no fear in his heart

A dervish performed his ablutions before prayer and unrolled his prayer rug. But he did not begin to pray, turning back instead and again, with still greater care, performing his ablutions. He returned to the room and knelt to pray, but again he did not begin, going to wash a third time.

Only after this third set of ablutions did he at last begin and complete his prayers. But for a long time still he continued to sit, drowning in tears and in grief.

102   *Wisdom of the Sufis*, pp. 59-60 (author's note).

The dervish's wife, observing from one side her husband's strange behavior, approached him some time later and asked why he had washed himself three separate times.

He answered, "In my heart there was no fear of the Lord God."

♦ ♦ ♦

His Holiness Sayyid Amir Kulal, may mercy be upon him, deigned to say, "If someone offends you, forgive him and ask no recompense... Be indifferent to the honor and the backbiting of people, lest you fall into the pit of perdition.

"If you are accosted by illness, be careful not to complain of the Lord Most High, but give praise and know that this sickness is atonement for your sins.

"And there is no ill that descends on a slave that is not a defense against some misfortune or sin.

"And if you are to be among people, listen carefully to all that they say about the *shari'at*, but if they speak in idleness, listen not at all.

"And if good should come to you from people, do not rejoice; but if they should speak ill of you, hold your tongue. Reward others in fairness, but do not demand fairness for yourself."

♦ ♦ ♦

My deceased mother, may mercy be upon her, once came home in tears and did not calm down for some time.

Everyone in the house tried to discover the reason for her tears, but she would just shake her head and continue to cry. She grew calm only after the mid-day prayers and then told what had happened on the road.

"I was coming from the marketplace," she began, and again pressed her eyes with the wet kerchief, "when a dog jumped out from behind a gate on a side street and started barking at me. I wouldn't have paid any attention to it, but it was mean and started to bite my dress hem. I didn't do anything to provoke it and didn't even try to drive it away. All I did was turn and look at it, and the dog suddenly gave a wild squeal, started to whine, and ran back through the gate. And there just inside was the owner of the house, who suddenly yelled after me, 'Witch!'"

At these words the tears again began to flow from her eyes, and she went on, "If God has even the slightest drop of compassion for me, He won't punish that man for offending me without thinking. Better let him reprimand me instead. I was the one who upset the poor animal after all."

◆ ◆ ◆

His Holiness Sayyid Amir Kulal, may mercy be upon him, admonished his followers thus:

"Act sincerely with all people and show them respect. Be abstemious, watch over your tongue in your relations with others. Do not let yourself be carried away, act meekly but not such that you make yourself worthless. Keep to the mean in all your actions, so said the Prophet, may Allah bless and greet him: 'Goodness in action is the mean.' Do not look at yourself, not even indirectly. Where there are many people, be with them, and, if you must speak, do so slowly, according to need."[103]

103 *Wisdom of the Sufis*, pp. 222-23 (author's note).

On Not Staring

The *murid* must not stare at the face of a *shaikh* during gatherings.

They tell the story of a poor man among the dervishes of Bahauddin Naqshband, may mercy be upon him, who looked constantly at his *shaikh* during discussions, and who was once told the following:

"There was once a man who would not take his eyes from the face of Hodja Bahauddin, may mercy be upon him. Our *hazrat*, may peace be upon him, said to the man, 'Do not look for too long into my face. You'll be lost.'"

✦ ✦ ✦

The *murid*, I think, probably needs to bring his abilities and his desires into accord. The fact that he demonstrates before everyone that he wants to take in a great deal from his *shaikh* all at once does not mean that his soul, the soul of the seeker, is in a condition to contain a great deal of divine light all at once. It will be like looking at the sun for a long time. A gaze directed at the shining sun may fill the soul with warmth and light, but that very light will blind one who takes it into his head to stare into it.

✦ ✦ ✦

They recount the story of how Shaikh Ali Romitani, may

his grave be sacred, was visited by one of his Sufis, whom the teacher greatly respected. It so happened that just then there was nothing at all in the *shaikh*'s house for rendering hospitality to his guest. He sat with his visitor and was terribly preoccupied. But very quickly a *murid* who had been dispatched brought some prepared food and placed it before the *shaikh*, bowing low in obedience, and saying, "I prepared this food for you. I hope you will accept it."

The *shaikh*'s face shone with joy when he saw the sincerity and obedience of his *murid*.

Guest and host ate. Then, when his visitor had left, Hazrat Ali Romitani, may mercy be upon him, called the youth and said to him, "May Allah bless you for your food, and may he accept your gift! Ask of me what you will, and you will receive it, God willing!"

In the soul of the youth lay too great a desire.

He said, "The limit of my desire is to resemble you, my *shaikh*, both in my appearance and in my manner of living!"

The *shaikh* grew thoughtful and then said, "This is something quite difficult. I'm afraid you might be unable to master it."

But the *murid* persisted in his desire and said, "I want nothing else!"

Then the *shaikh* took him by the hand, and led him into the mystical state of *halvatun*, [104] directing onto him all the force of his spiritual energy, favoring him according to the persistence of his request.

104 *Halvatun*: a place of isolation or secret conversation of the Sufis with God (author's note).

An hour later the youth came out of the mystical state. He resembled his *shaikh* in external appearance and in his manner of behavior. No one could distinguish one from the other. The youth lived another forty days, but Sufis maintain that the poor man lived even less than that.

On Concentration

In the presence of his *shaikh*, the *murid* must not think of peripheral things; entrusting himself to the *shaikh*, he should sit with lowered head and downcast eyes.

I sit in the *hanaqa*, listening to the wise council of my *shaikh* and trying to concentrate on his enlightened heart, and I feel my veneration for him flooding my soul and a dull shroud of mist covering my eyes. Next to me, his head lowered to his chest, another *murid* sits, and his eyes too shine with a dull, watery sheen.

"What does my soul lament?" I ask myself, and find no immediate answer, only a sense of peacefulness and tranquility that spreads through my entire body. Yes, tranquility—from the realization that I who have been such a wretched man, sunk in the filth of my sins and doubts, am at this moment faithfully protected by my *shaikh* from everything doubtful and sinful, everything accidental and hopeless.

Who was I before meeting my *hazrat*? A helpless, weak lamb lost in the endless steppe, pitifully bellowing and looking round in search of its mother.

Where have my previous dismay and uncertainty about tomorrow gone? Here in the *hanaqa*, I feel that I am defended from the random storms of my previously ill-defined life. Neither doubts nor words remain. It's as if they never were, neither the doubts, nor the excessive words.

There is only a quiet and bright joy, like the pure water of a spring whose waves roll onto my heart with each glance of my *shaikh* upon me.

God entrusted me to my *shaikh*, and now I needn't fear anything. My only anxiety is learning not to think. My subjective mental activity is bounded in time and space, and for that very reason did such activity insert in my life such dismay and doubt, impatience and displeasure with myself.

In the course of my relatively long life I managed to stuff my soul with such a quantity of trash that now I think only about succeeding in cleansing it. My tears here in the *hanaqa* are grief over the purity that was once in my heart, which I myself betrayed out of forgetfulness, like a patch of neglected land, grown thick with weeds.

My tears are grief over the many years of a Godless life wasted in making my heart numb, wild, and cruel.

God does not come to that place, I think, recalling someone's words, where there is the least hint of filth.

I look upon my *shaikh*, and my heart fills with a quiet light of gratitude that I make no effort to hide.

On Proper Frame of Mind

One must absolutely avoid thinking of the visit to one's *shaikh* as an amusement or pleasurable pastime; one must come to the *shaikh* with the express purpose of receiving instruction needed in the doctrine of the *tariqat* and in general for leading a devout life.

The *hanaqa* is a sacred place for the Sufi. Its holiness is palpable in the trees that grow in the courtyard and in the water one drinks, not merely in the rooms where discussions and prayer take place. Each stone that has been placed in the courtyard has felt on its back the blessed steps of many upon many enlightened figures, who have devoted their lives to the service of the Lord.

✦ ✦ ✦

Abu Huraira, may mercy be upon him, says:

> A meeting in which Allah is remembered shines
> amidst heavenly creation in exactly the same way
> that the stars shine for earthly creatures.

✦ ✦ ✦

The messenger of Allah, may Allah bless and greet him, says in one of his *ahadith*:

When some group of people recollects Allah in
their meeting, angels surround the assembly, and
the mercy of Allah descends upon the people, and
Allah refers to them in the councils of the angels.

+ + +

They say that Shaikh Allauddin Attar, may Allah
be pleased with him, was one of the favorite pupils of
Bahauddin Naqshband, may mercy be upon him. His
father left three sons upon his death. Allaudin Attar divided his inheritance between his brothers, refusing
earthly goods for himself, in favor of study at the Bukhara
medresse. He was talented in all branches of learning and
attained unheard of heights in them.

Bahauddin Naqshband, may his grave be sacred, had a
little daughter, and he said to the girl's mother, "When our
daughter grows up, inform me!"

When the girl had reached maturity, the mother informed her husband, and Shaikh Bahauddin set out for
the Bukhara medresse where Shaikh Allauddin Attar was
engaged in study.

When Shaikh Bahauddin entered his room, he found
nothing there but a ragged blouse on which Allauddin
slept, a brick, which he used as a pillow, and a broken vase,
by means of which he performed his ablutions.

When he saw all this, Shaikh Bahauddin Naqshband
fell at the feet of Allauddin Attar, may his grave be sacred,
kissing them and placing his forehead upon them. Then
he said to Shaikh Allauddin: "I have a daughter who just

reached maturity. And today the Most High and Beneficent Allah has commanded me to give her to you in marriage."

Shaikh Allauddin responded, "This is a great joy to me. The Great and Almighty Allah has gladdened me. But I own nothing with which to sustain the expenses of keeping a family, and as for my state of affairs, you have seen."

Shaikh Bahauddin said, "What Allah destined to each of you for your daily bread will come to you if Allah so pleases! Do not even think about that...."

And he gave her to him in marriage, concluding a marriage pact. After the newlyweds' first night together, Shaikh Bahauddin ordered Shaikh Allauddin to leave the medresse, gave him a large tray piled with apples, and told him to place the tray on his head and walk barefoot around the squares and marketplaces of Bukhara, calling out loudly, "Apples, apples!" until he had sold them all.

Shaikh Allauddin placed the tray on his head, went to the marketplace, and began to call out, "Apples, apples!"

When his two brothers, who occupied important positions in society, saw this, they were filled with anger against him for his behavior. Shaikh Bahauddin Naqshband learned of their outrage and told Shaikh Allauddin to take the tray with the apples, place it close to the stands of his brothers, and sell them there. Shaikh Allauddin did exactly as he had been ordered by Shaikh Bahauddin, trading in apples for a long time afterward, while Shaikh Bahauddin taught him the silent *zikr*.

✦ ✦ ✦

Allauddin Attar, may mercy be upon him, said:

"The *murid* must disclose his mystical states to his *shaikh* in the conviction that he will attain his true and authentic goal only thanks to the good favor of his *pir*. Therefore must the *murid* seek the good will of his *shaikh*, believing that until a given moment all doors to the truth, visible and invisible, except that which is his *murshid*, will remain closed to him. He must bring himself in sacrifice to his teacher.

"The sign of a complete and ideal *murid* lies in his recognition of the fact that no matter how much ordinary religious knowledge or secret knowledge he may possess, no matter how great is the yearning and diligence he may manifest on the path to God, he will find not even a trace of authentic knowledge in himself. In his eyes all such knowledge is like a speck of dust in comparison with what his mentor knows."

❖ ❖ ❖

Since I entrusted all my affairs, both worldly and religious, to the will and keeping of my *shaikh*, it is as if a heavy weight has slipped from my shoulders. I was like a mountain stream pounding and tearing at its banks, and then, suddenly, I found myself in a valley, where the course was markedly slower and a quiet appeasement came to rest upon my shoulders.

Sufis say that the *murid* must not retain even the slightest bit of his own will. Only one who constantly sees the inadequacy of his strivings on the path to God may hope for success or benefit, who considers himself an unfinished person, who seeks refuge in the magnanimity and mercy of the Lord of worlds.

Part Three

Rules of the Gathering

On Joining With Others

When moving from isolation to the meeting proper, it is necessary that one truly desire to join those present and not be guided by some ulterior motive.

We read about what the *murid* should be like in the *Kabusname*[105]:

> The dervish should always demonstrate submis
> sion before God; he must never disclose his
> thoughts to anyone from among the brothers.[106][...]
>
> His zeal should always be directed toward con-
> sidering his brothers as better than him, and self-
> love should be banished from his head. [...]
>
> He must not have personal goals. He must set
> them aside. His glance must be both one of renun-
> ciation and confirmation, but he must look upon
> nothing with ambivalence. [...]
>
> He must allow neither preconceptions nor dis-
> agreements to enter his glance. For looking without
> preconceptions is itself a confirmation. No one will
> contradict him, for the essence of truth is the denial
> of ambivalence, the essence of sincerity the denial of
> contradiction. [...]

105   *Kabusname* (also *Qabusnamah*): eleventh-century book of moral instruction by Unsur al-Maali Kaykavus ibn Iskandar ibn Qabus (d. 1098).

106   His thoughts concerning his mystical states (author's note).

If one with full sincerity steps onto the water, the water grows firm beneath his foot.... Once you have recognized true sincerity, do not deny it but take it on faith, for sincerity is a phenomenon that neither reason nor force can deposit in your heart. If it is to be placed inside you, it will come only through a gift of the Lord Most High and Glorious. [...]

The dervish is one with the gaze of sincerity. He makes no habit out of fear, and his exterior and interior are alike. His heart is not empty of ruminations on unity, but he prefers a certain slowness in his thoughts, lest he be consumed by the fire of contemplation. For the people of the *tariqat* have seen that contemplation is like a fire, for which consolation is the quenching water. [107]

✦ ✦ ✦

I am a *murid*. And nothing should issue from a *murid*, say the *shaikhs* of the Hadjagon Tariqat, that might serve as a reason for denying the thoughts of the *shaikhs*. But how can a simple man like me attain such a level that my desires should be the desires of my *shaikh* and his should become mine? This, say the Sufis, is one of the paths of a person's ennoblement. And by such a path one attains happiness.

---

107   Unsur al-Maali. *Kabus-name*. In *Zvezda Vostoka (Star of the East)*, Nos. 3-4 (1994), pp. 20-21 (author's note).

On Ritual Washing

Before a gathering it is essential that one perform one's ablutions; beforehand one should wash and scent one's clothing and body; ill-scented objects should be put aside so as not to cause unpleasantness for those in attendance. One should brush one's teeth and rid the mouth of the odor of raw onions, garlic, and the like, so as not to arouse the displeasure of those attending the gathering.

On the manner of the *murid*'s behavior, the *Kabusname* says the following:

> *If a dervish has no internal education, he should at least have external education, so that of these two he should at least be covered with an external form* . . . .
>
> A *murid* must not wear the clothing of his *pir*, nor the shoes. He mustn't sit in the *pir*'s place or drink from a vessel prepared for him. He mustn't sleep before him or perform the *namaz*[108] while the *pir* is looking. He must love his *shaikh* more than even than his children or parents. This love, Sufi tradition maintains, is an indispensable condition of joy in both worlds . . . .
>
> He must not enter the *hanaqa* by himself, for sins arise from solitude. And when he has entered,

---

108   *Namaz*: series of ritual activities including posture, body position, dress, movement, and prayer formulas (author's note).

he must not hinder anyone. He should first take off his left shoe. When leaving he should first put on his right ....

He should make use of every opportunity to wash his hands. With others he should not rush, before them he should not pace. Let him not sit in another's place, or be over sensitive ....

In youth the dervish should consider work as a treasure. In old age he should elect for slowness. During the taking of food he should not absent himself from the table, lest others wait for him. He should not be first to extend his hand to the food nor first to finish his meal, except with the assent of others. He should not desire more than he is given ....

If he is unable to eat because of illness, he should excuse himself before the table is set. He should not talk over his food. If he is fasting and the table is set, he should not speak of his fast and may break it."[109]

+ + +

His Holiness Amir Kulal, may mercy be upon him, deigned to say:

Until you have burned everything that you have, you will never become truly happy.

109   *Kabusname*, pp. 21-23 (author's note).

This means that until the *murid* rids himself of all his harmful habits and bad character traits, until he burns all that distances him from God in the fire of Godly worship, he will never be able to cleanse his heart and approach the understanding of Truth.

His Holiness Amir Kulal also frequently said to his followers:

"If your back is not bent like a bow from prayer and your body doesn't become as thin as the bow's string, you will never reach the greatness and glory of the Creator. The basis of everything is following Him. *He who has chosen a path in opposition to the Prophet will never reach his halting place!*"

The Qur'anic phrase *"and cleanse thy garments"* is a confirmation of these words. If some commentators have claimed that the meaning of this is the maintenance of clean clothing, others have insisted that it means having proper moral disposition.

For with the proper disposition a person, especially a person attempting to make his way on the path to Truth, can attain any goal or aspiration. After all, his Holiness our Prophet, may our prayer and peace be upon him, had many positive traits, but the Lord of the World, may remembrance of Him be glorified for there is no other god but Him, called his disposition great.

On Proper Posture

At gatherings one should behave with decency, sitting respectfully and making sure not to cause anyone around one discomfort; one mustn't allow one's knees to rest atop the knees of one's neighbor, nor sit between two people without their permission.

Malik ibn Anas, may mercy be upon him, told the following story:

"If anyone came to the Prophet, may Allah bless and greet him, and took his hand in greeting, the Prophet, the peace and blessing of Allah be his, never removed his hand from his interlocutor's first. Nor was he ever the first to turn away. And at meetings, he never stretched out his legs before those present, such that they might be even slightly ahead of the knees of those sitting beside him."[110]

---

110 *Hadith* handed down by al-Bukhari (author's note).

On Remembering God

While sitting at a gathering, one must remember God incessantly.

God the Most High says:

"Remember Me, and I shall remember you." [111]

That is, His Holiness the Most High Lord tells us to maintain a mental image of His greatness in our hearts, and then He will remember us with goodness.

It is not God who takes away our share of the light, but we who do ourselves out of it. It is not God who indicates to us the crooked and long path to Him, but we ourselves who wander in the gloom of our sinful ways and actions, our immorality and egoism. But the moment we grow the least bit ashamed of our life, God rushes to meet us.

The All High says:

"And when you have completed your prayers, remember Allah—while standing, sitting, or lying down." [112]

By this the Lord wished to say that those who wish to be

---

111 Qur'an 2:152.
112 Qur'an 4:103.

greatly favored by the All High must not limit themselves to the required prayers. It is, in essence, a direct reference to Sufi practice and to that of all righteous people, whom He councils to continue their remembrance and glorification of God wherever they might be and whatever their physical position—"standing, sitting, or lying down."

+ + +

It is recounted from the words of Malik ibn Anas, may Allah be pleased with him, that in conveying the words of the Great and Almighty Lord, the Prophet, may Allah bless and greet him, said:

> If a slave comes nearer to Me by a finger's breadth, I shall come to him by a cubit; if he comes nearer by a cubit, I shall come to him by a stride; and if he should begin walking toward Me, I shall hurry to him at a run![113]

+ + +

Thoughts, memories, and conversations in the *hanaqa* concern God alone. Everything earthly moves involuntarily to the background, growing muffled and dull, as though all that remained outside the gates of the sacred home of the Sufis were indeed secondary. And there are only gentle, subdued voices, a cordiality and warmth of regard, and the

---

113   *Hadith* handed down by al-Bukhari (author's note).

wise words of the *shaikh*, which penetrate into the depth of the heart, disturbing it, causing it suffering and compassion, while pure, unbidden tears quietly splash outside.

In the *hanaqa* one thinks of God. And God is recollected in words.

✦ ✦ ✦

According to the testimonial of Abu Abbas Abdullah,[114] son of Abbas, may mercy be upon him, who said:

"I once sat beside the Prophet, may Allah bless him and send him peace, and he said:

"'You man! I shall teach you several precepts.

"'Remember Allah and Allah will protect you; remember Allah and you will see Him before you.

"'If you should ask, ask of Allah; if you seek aid, seek the aid of Allah.

"'Know that if the people should gather to do great favor unto you, they do such favor only for what Allah has allotted to you; know that if the people should gather to injure you, they injure only that which Allah has allotted to you. The pen has risen from the paper, and the ink on the pages has dried.'"[115]

In a different version than that of at-Tirmidhi, it is written:

---

114   Abu Abbas Abdullah (also, Abdullah ibn Abbas, d. 689): cousin of the Prophet Muhammad.

115   That is, "what is written cannot be altered." Cited by at-Tirmidhi (author's note).

Remember Allah and you will see Him before you.
Know Allah in well being, and He will know you
in need.
Know that what has passed you by was not meant
for you and that what has happened to you was not
meant to pass you by.
And know that there is no victory without patience,
no relief without hardship, and nothing found
without loss.

+ + +

The time for prayer is approaching, and I stand with the
other *murids* in order to renew our ablutions. As I leave
the room, I see a young *murid* straightening the shoes of
the Sufis so that they might find them and put them on
without difficulty upon coming out.

I thank him with a nod, while he, favored with the
thanks of a brother, smiles back.

When I arrive at the place where jugs of water have
been placed for washing, another brother hands me a jug
filled with warm water, bowing slightly. I am thankful to
God that He has brought such a simple man as me into a
brotherhood of attentive, tactful people, and I smile to the
dervish, who responds in kind.

+ + +

It is said that Abu Bakr, may Allah be pleased with

him, often shed tears from the strength of his righteous contemplation. Once he asked for water for his ablutions, and he was brought a vessel. He performed his ablutions and broke into tears. Those around him also began to cry. He cried amid the sound of sobbing all around. After some time he came to himself and washed his face with cold water.

"What brought you to such a state," they asked him. "We thought you were going to die."

Abu Bakr responded: "I was once with the chosen one Muhammad, may Allah bless and greet him, and saw that he was pushing something away, saying, 'Away, away from me!' I saw no one beside him and asked who it was he was driving from him.

"And the Prophet responded, 'This world (*ad-dun'ia*) [116] had stood up before me with all that is in it, and I cried out and threatened it.

"'The world jumped away from me and answered, 'No one besides you will be able to do without me!'"

"And I suddenly grew frightened," concluded Abu Bakr, "that the world would overtake me. And that provoked my tears."

◆ ◆ ◆

Our predecessors were profoundly conscious of the

---

116   In the eyes of Muslims, especially the Sufis, the world (*ad-dun'ia*) incarnates the false, transient temptations and delusions that lead a person away from the righteous path (author's note).

sinfulness and baseness of the earthly world. They realized that the soul's inveiglement depended upon the weakness of human nature and its capacity for evil. About this it is said in the *hadith*:

"According to the testimonial of Abu al Abbas Sahl ibn Sa'ad as-Sayyid, may mercy be upon him, who said:

"'A man came to the Prophet, may Allah bless and greet him, and said:

"'O Messenger of God, show me the action I may perform that will cause Allah to love me and the people to love me.'

"'He said: 'Renounce the world and Allah will love you. Renounce what the people possess and the people will love you.'"" [117]

❖ ❖ ❖

Boyazid Bistami, [118] may mercy be upon him, said:

"At the start of my Sufi path I was mistaken in four things: I supposed that it was I who prayed to and glorified Him, that it was I who knew Him, loved Him, and sought Him. But when I looked into it more carefully, I discovered that His prayers about me, His knowledge of me, His love for me, and His seeking after me, all preceded my first appeal to Him."

❖ ❖ ❖

117   Conveyed by ibn Majah (d. 887) (author's note).
118   Boyazid Bistami (also Abu Yazid al-Bistami, d. 875).

The Sufi is in a state of constant meditation. Whatever his hands might do, whomever he might speak with or meet, the Sufi constantly remembers God in accordance with the principle of the Naqshbandi Tariqat:

> May your hands be busy with the affairs of the world while your heart remembers God.

And here is a poor man like me, whose attention wanders and is forever drawn to worldly things, and I wonder how I am ever to attain such a height that the problems of the world should seem as nothing to me in comparison with the thoughts of God.

It seems to me that before the All High Lord directed me to the *hanaqa*, my soul resembled an unbroken horse, proud of its unbridled external beauty. What use to a person is such garish and fiery beauty? A clotted fusion of monstrous strength, of passion condensed to an extreme. One admires it, and that's that.

Only a horse that is tame and obedient, a horse with a gentle disposition, obtains worth in the eyes of man. And so, observing myself from one side, I learn how to tame my disposition. And the more I think about my *shaikh*, the more I attempt to duplicate his experience; the more compliant and obedient my soul becomes, the more gentleness and humility I find in my heart.

◆ ◆ ◆

Shaikh Bahauddin, may mercy be upon him, once asked his supporters:

"Whom may one call a *fakir*? [119]

No one responded. Then he said:

> The fakir is one whose interior is war and
> whose exterior is peace.

+ + +

Hazrat Bahauddin Naqshband, may his grave be sacred, said:

"Sometimes the *talib*, or 'beginning Sufi,' must neglect the performance of the *nafil namaz*, [120] in order that they not turn into a mechanical and senseless habit, should he grow accustomed to them. For the goal of the recitation of prayers is the Sufi's contact with the Lord God, not with the ritual actions themselves. For this reason did the Prophet Muhammad, may Allah bless and greet him, say:

> The joy of my eyes is found in prayer.

He did not say that this joy was contained in the mere recitation of prayer.

+ + +

119   *Fakir*: Sufi (author's note).
120   *Nafil namaz*: supplemental prayers recited by the Sufi most commonly at night (author's note).

From the lips of our Shaikh Ibrahim, may the mercy of Allah be upon him, I heard the story of how some young *murids*, through inexperience and carelessness, violated an unwritten law of the *hanaqa* and were shamed as a result.

Once Hodja Ahrar Vali, may mercy be upon him, passed into the part of the *hanaqa* where *murids* usually warm water for ablutions, where he happened to overhear his followers in idle conversation. The *hazrat* approached them and said:

"It saddens me to think of the lot of the man who washes with that water."

What is there to say then, I thought sadly, about *murids* who carry on conversations as if they were on the street while warming up the water? And I recalled the words of our *hazrat*, which he uttered at the end of the story:

"Our path is difficult. But the Merciful One does not merely bring the person into the *hanaqa*, He gives him strength for making progress along that very path. What is required from us is constant watchfulness and the consciousness of each instant. The moment we lose our vigilance, then and there we begin to slide from the mountain on which we found ourselves just before."

✦ ✦ ✦

In the *Biographies of the Saints*, Hazrat Farid ad-Din Attar,[121] may mercy be upon him, tells the story of how

121 Farid ad-Din Attar (d. ca. 1220): Persian mystic poet.

Shaikh Ja'far Sadiq, [122] may his grave be made holy, once turned to his *murid* Boyazid Bistami with a request to get him a certain book from the shelf.

"What shelf?" asked his pupil.

"You've been a *murid* for so long already," said the *shaikh*, reprimanding him slightly, "and still haven't seen the bookshelf?"

"I did not come here out of idle curiosity," answered Bistami, "not to be examining the four walls of the *hanaqa*."

These words of the young *murid* pleased the *shaikh* so much that he immediately said, "Well, Boyazid! You may consider your education complete. Go back home to your Bistam!"

✦ ✦ ✦

My deceased mother, may mercy be upon her, was a deeply religious, god-fearing woman. Near the end of her life she grew calm and reticent. And she cried very much. She cried while she performed her ablutions, during her prayers, in between them.

When my two sisters spoke even about things that were most urgent, she would suddenly tell them, "Stop jabbering! Don't you fear God!?"

"We do," her daughters would say, hesitating, "but we have to take care of these problems too."

And once I overheard Mama explaining why she wasn't pleased with my sisters' "jabbering."

122   Ja'far Sadiq (d. 765): theologian, jurist; spiritual initiator of Bistami.

"How can you not understand!?" she said with fervor. "All our thoughts that don't contain God, all our words that aren't about Him, are completely empty. They weigh no more than a speck of dust that the wind carries from one unknown place to another.

"Your grandmother," she continued, "told me that a day that passed without mention of the Lord God's name is erased by Him from that person's consciousness. And if days like that build up in a person, then before his death, lying on his death-bed, he tries to recall his life but can't.

"He can't remember the woman who lived with him all his conscious life, and now, shedding tears, stands before him as he dies. He doesn't remember the children who surround him. He can't remember them because he lived without God in his soul, like a beast, and without God in his soul he dies. Nothing remains in his memory. Nothing, not God, not he himself, the man. Everything's been erased...."

I was little then and couldn't stand women crying, which is why, when Mama's story came to the end, I ran out into the street. For the tears of three women is already a river.

A Strange Method of Instruction

There once lived a Sufi who instructed his pupils through discussion, but also through numerous methods that his followers found unexpected. One of his students was a *salik*, a Sufi at the start of his path to God, who was known for his extreme absent-mindedness, which hindered him from concentrating on God. It sometimes happened that, seated in the *hanaqa*, he would suddenly start to think about something else and would smile where others were weeping. The *shaikh* saw this but waited for the proper moment in order to teach his pupil a lesson.

And once the *murid* came to his teacher and spoke openly. "*Hazrat*," he said, lowering his head, "my prayers do not bring me satisfaction."

"Because during them," said his *shaikh*, "you are distracted by other thoughts."

"I'm not distracted," said the *murid* uncertainly.

"We shall see about that."

And with these words the Sufi took up a truncheon prepared in advance for this occasion and began to strike his pupil with it.

The stunned dervish jumped away and began running around the room, trying to evade the blows. But no matter where he turned, the *shaikh*'s truncheon reached him. The *shaikh* put all his effort into striking his pupil, and the latter tried still harder to evade the blows.

Tired by swinging the truncheon at last, the Sufi threw it to one side and sat down.

The *salik*, who had been driven into a corner by the blows of his mentor, continued to stand tensely.

"Be seated!" commanded the Sufi.

The *murid* sat down in silence, favoring his left arm, which had been struck more often.

"What were you thinking about when I was trying to hit you?" asked the *shaikh*.

"About saving myself," the *murid* admitted.

"Only that?"

"Only that, teacher."

"When you learn to think only about God during your prayers," said the *hazrat* to his follower, "then they will bring you satisfaction."

✦ ✦ ✦

At sunrise after morning prayer, a Sufi was reading the great *surah* from the Yasin, or heart, of the Qur'an. When he reached the mid-point, his glance happened to fall on his legs and then, from one side, on himself: he was not kneeling on a prayer rug but was seated on a comfortable divan, his legs crossed before him. The Sufi's consciousness went dark. Fear rushed down his spine. Incapable of holding back his sobs, he rushed to perform his ablutions anew. Still sobbing, he returned to the room and recited two *rak'at*, [123] repenting before God for his lack of attentiveness, and only then returned to reading the great *surah*.

Pray Alone

"*Hazrat*, what am I to do?" asked a *talib* of his teacher. "Thoughts constantly distract me during prayer."

"Pray alone!" the Sufi advised.

The man went home and told his wife about his

---

123 *Rak'at*: prayer cycle.

conversation with the *shaikh*, adding seriously, "And from today you will pray in a separate room from me."

"Fine!" said his wife, laughing. "But when your *pir* advised you to pray alone, he had something completely different in mind."

"And what was that?" he asked.

"He meant that even as you perform your ablutions you should have left all outside thoughts behind, and then, if God should so desire, you shall receive satisfaction in your prayers."

A Conversation

"How am I to learn to be silent, like all wise men?"

"Fill your heart with love."

"What can I do so that with every inward and outward breath I yearn for God?"

"Fill your heart with love."

"But what am I to do to be worthy of the Beloved's favor?"

"Weep!"

On Improper Speech

One should be careful of pronouncing unseemly words during a gathering, or of showing ugly aspects of one's character, or making improper gestures.

Boyazid Bistami, may mercy be upon him, said:

"Once in the dead of night, I stretched out my legs in the *mihrab*. [124] And then I heard the secret voice of God:

'He who sits in the company of kings sits only by observing decorum.'"

+ + +

An associate of Bahauddin Naqshband, may mercy be upon him, told a story that has come down to us as follows:

"When I had just been vouchsafed the honor of becoming an associate of Shaikh Bahauddin, may Allah be pleased with him, Shaikh Shadi, one of his most prominent students, would often read me edifying words, give me council, and educate me. One of his instructions was a prohibition against any of us sitting with our legs stretched in the direction of Shaikh Bahauddin.

"On one occasion I arrived in the *hanaqa* when it was very

---

124   *Mihrab*: a sanctuary inside the mosque (which points in the direction that the praying person must turn his face) (author's note).

hot, and I took shelter in the shade of one of the courtyard trees, where I lay down on the ground. An animal came up to me and twice bit me on the foot. It was terribly painful, but again I lay down. The animal approached and bit me a third time. I sat up and thought for some time about why this had happened, until I remembered the advice of Shaikh Shadi and realized that I had stretched out my feet in the direction of the lodge, where Shaikh Bahauddin was at the time. Then I understood that what had happened was a correction of my inattentive behavior."

On Humility

It is improper to try and stand out amid others by show-ing one's ability to concentrate or the degree of one's spiri-tual accomplishment; on the contrary, one should conceal one's significance in humility. If during a gathering you are able to engage in reading a book or in some devout conversation about the faith, do so; but if not, engage in something else, concealing the degree of your spiritual ac-complishment.

Obedience, humility, and modesty—these are the cri-teria of a man's greatness, so Sufis believe. To one who is humble and modest even enemies cannot be the cause of evil. Human self-importance often counterpoises such qualities. It makes its appearance even amid the Sufi lodge—the *hanaqa*.

✦ ✦ ✦

They say that Hasan Basri, [125] may mercy be upon him, had a *murid* who would lie face down on the ground each time he heard verses from the Qur'an. On one occasion Hasan Basri said to him:

"If you are able to not do what you're doing, then, man, for your whole life you've just been fanning the hellish fire

---

125   Hasan al-Basri (d. 728 or 737): Arab theologian and scholar of Islam; one of the greatest Sufis of the Middle East (author's note).

by your behavior. But if you're incapable of not acting thus, then you've outstripped me ten times over."

Then he said, "Thunder comes from the evil spirit. From each person who utters a loud exclamation, it comes from none other than the evil spirit. If a man is capable of suppressing a loud exclamation but nevertheless utters it anyway, it comes from none other than the evil spirit."[126]

◆ ◆ ◆

I once witnessed a scene in the *hanaqa* in which a Sufi, demonstrating the degree of his spiritual accomplishment and advancement along the path, sat reveling in his ability to immerse himself in God. May the Most High forgive me if, through my ignorance, I slander my brother. It is entirely possible that this was the natural state of an experienced *murid*, capable of distancing himself from his surroundings, but his self-immersion had a negative effect on the *talib*. It naturally provoked the thought: *I am not able to do that.*

◆ ◆ ◆

They tell the story that Amir Kulal, may his grave be sacred, was once in the village of Hodja Mubarak, while Hodja Bahauddin, may mercy be upon him, was in the service of Amir Kulal. The *hodja* suddenly thought:

126 *Sufism in the Context of Muslim Culture* (Russian). Moscow, 1989, pp. 159-60 (author's note).

"No one is closer to his Holiness Amir Kulal than I."

At just that moment a man came to Amir Kulal with a request, leading an enormous sheep as a gift.

"It would be good if Maulana Arif Diggarani were here so he could roast that sheep," thought the *hodja*, upon which his Holiness Amir Kulal said,

"Bahauddin, rise and tell Maulana Arif to come here."

The *hodja* responded, "But *Hazrat*, we're in the province of Nasaf, and the maulana is in the province of Karmin. How am I to tell him?"

His Holiness Amir Kulal said, "You needn't go anywhere. Simply go outside and say, 'O, Maulana Arif!'"

The *hodja* went outside, stood at the corner of the house, and three times said, "Maulana Arif!"

Hodja Bahauddin had barely sat down again inside when Maulana Arif entered, greeted them, and said, "Bahauddin, did his Holiness tell you to call me three times?"

Bahauddin was astounded, but his Holiness Amir Kulal said, "Child Bahauddin, there have been those who were closer to me than you. Try not to allow yourself improper thoughts, and do not observe yourself and your own affairs. There is nothing worse in a man than self-importance."

And on this the following *rubai*:

> The veil of self-importance before you,
> Take it away and you'll see a living face.
> Iblis suffered for his self-importance.
> Be careful, my brother, in your earthly hour. [127]

127 *Wisdom of the Sufis*, pp. 96-97 (author's note).

✦ ✦ ✦

Sufis say that those who boast of their immersion in the mystical states are deprived by God of His favor, for the path of love is above all the path of humility and obedience, and the Sufi hasn't the right to tell others about that which only God or his *hazrat* may relate to him.

✦ ✦ ✦

Once at a meeting of the *murids* and followers of Shaikh Ubaydullah Ahrar Vali, may mercy be upon him, a *murid* sat with his head bowed low to bury himself in contemplation. The *shaikh* grew angry with him and said,

"One man sat just like you at a gathering of our Shaikh Nizameddin Khamush, may Allah be pleased with him. And Hazrat Nizameddin said to him,

"'Raise your head! I see smoke coming from your mouth. It's still early for you to be plunging into the contemplation of God and your mystical states! First you must carry water and pebbles for the *istinj*, [128] clean the latrines over the course of many years, before preparing yourself to have the right to immerse yourself in the mystical condition."

128 *Istinj*: cleansing with small clay pebbles after a movement of the bowels (author's note).

On Reticence

Don't talk too much. The teachers of the *tariqat* council us to speak only when the soul is obedient to the tongue and the tongue is obedient to God, which means only with sincerity. For one who has just entered a gathering it is best to keep absolute silence.

Ibn Abu Hala [129] said, "The silence of Allah's Messenger, may Allah bless and greet him, expresses patience, perspicacity, thoughtfulness, and contemplation."

♦ ♦ ♦

Shaikh Bahauddin, may Allah be pleased with him, told the following story:

"Shaikh Abu Said ibn Abi al-Khair, [130] may Allah be pleased with him, said that maintaining the image of the *shaikh* in his heart but visiting his teacher rarely is better for the *murid* than being constantly in the *shaikh's* presence without such an image."

And Bahauddin Naqshband, may mercy be upon him, also said:

"It is essential that in the course of the *shaikh's* accom-

129 Abu Hala (d. 689): Companion of the Prophet Muhammad.
130 Abu Said ibn Abi al-Khair (d. 1049): Persian poet, first composer of *rubaiyat*.

paniment the hardships that fall to the *murid* be such that he can carry them out, so that he does not lose faith in the *shaikh*. If the *murid* is one who has experience with the immersion in the mystical condition, then he need no longer ask questions of his mentor."

The Wordlessness of the Present

A *salik*, or traveler on the mystic path, came to his *shaikh* and asked the meaning of the phrase, "Before the Sufi can speak, he must learn to be silent."

"Go into the next room and think," said the *shaikh* to his pupil. "I'll summon you in a while."

The *murid* wanted to ask his *shaikh* what else he should think about but changed his mind. He immediately rose, betook himself to the next room, and began to consider. At first he thought about God; then remembered his wife who was just then due to deliver and began to think about her. He went through names in his head in order to choose a worthy one for his future son. He wanted a son. Then he remembered God again and began mechanically using the prayer beads in his hands. The thought that soon he would need money again caused him to forget about God.

Just then he was called back to his *shaikh*, who said to him:

"When we continue to count on ourselves, we start to rush about. We chase after our thoughts of the past, while they rush into the future. We open the still empty rooms of the future, but our thoughts are back in the past once more. And all the time we are chasing them, we lose our present. But God, He is here and now, and every instant lived without Him is yet another lost possibility for finding joy in the depth and brightness of that moment.

"This is why I tell you," continued the *shaikh*, "to learn how to immerse yourself in the wordlessness of the present. It will become the past without you. The more you plunge yourself into the divine wordlessness of the present, the more senseless will the thoughts that tormented you yesterday seem.

"The moment of your soul in which God was not present is now hopelessly lost to you. Learn to be silent about everything unconnected with the name of God and then, perhaps, He will one day teach your tongue sincerity. For in the Qur'an it is said:

> *They utter with their tongues what is not in the hearts.* [131]

Color suffused the cheeks of the *murid* who had asked his question, and he bent his head low.

+ + +

I now recall with gratitude one of my brothers, with whom I used to be in the habit of visiting the *hanaqa* of our *shaikh*. Every time I was burning to ask Hazrat Ibrahim about something, he would give me a gentle prod

---

131   Qur'an 48:11.

of the elbow on my hand, invisible to others, and I would be compelled to swallow the question that would have, it seemed, drawn the attention of everyone, and particularly that of my *shaikh*, to me. And if at first the thorn pricked my self-esteem, after some two hours, when I had become conscious of the emptiness and worthlessness of my unasked question, I would be grateful to him.

The most surprising part was that this brother would never bring up the awkwardness that I had created. Only once, when we'd remained alone, he quite gently and politely said:

"If you want to ask the *shaikh* a question, wait first. Let it grow in your heart. Give it time so that you can see with perspective how profound and important it is. If after several hours you still want to ask the *shaikh*, go ahead. But I suspect there will be no need: our *shaikh* always answers all the questions that have arisen in the hearts of his *murids*."

This became a lesson to me, and afterward, when the desire to pose a question would arise in my soul, I no longer even had to suppress it. Like a beaten dog, it would rush away the moment I directed my glance inward.

A Conversation

"Teacher, doubts overwhelm me."
"Then be silent."
"But what will silence give me?"
"Perhaps you'll grow ashamed."

"Of what?"

"Of the fact that each word not directed toward God becomes a quiet nest for the grim song bird of doubt."

Stop Watching Yourself

"I've been coming to the *hanaqa* for a whole year," said one *murid* to another, "and I've never been able to figure out for myself why some *murids* listen to the *shaikh's* discussions in silence and shed tears, while with me if I listen carefully to the words, my heart does not keep up with them."

"Stop watching the others!" the *shaikh* once said to me. Some time passed, but little changed within me.

"Stop watching yourself!" the *shaikh* told me.

A third admonition was unnecessary.

♦ ♦ ♦

An ordinary man becomes the slave of his illusory "I." At first, when the man is still young, his *nafs* glances inside him, sees him as master, but verifies how quickly the youth carries out each desiring impulse. Then, seeing the man become more and more pleased to follow its lead, the *nafs* itself becomes master.

At precisely this point the character of the *nafs* changes. If before it was gentle and not especially demanding, now it becomes tough, perfidious, and sneaky. It thrusts implausible desires into the heart of its former master as into a burning furnace, and these ignite it and deprive it of sleep and peace until he should fulfill them. The man burns in a flame of unfulfilled desires. They blaze within, rising ever higher until he is completely enslaved by his insatiable *nafs*.

And now, driven onward by the new master, the man looks into its eyes, cringing and wriggling before it, obliging it in every conceivable manner, only in order to satisfy the irrepressible passion of his ego. And the more the man obliges his *nafs*, the more inflexible and merciless becomes the egoistic animal.

The *nafs* increases in size, inflating like a great balloon, while behind it the man is no longer visible at all: the more he obliges his desires and passions, the less of the human being remains within him. The *nafs* grows, the man shrinks.

And it is no longer the man that towers above the well-placed functionary in the soft leather arm chair. It's his inordinately inflated vainglory. He begins to see the entire world through the prism of his unfulfilled desires, where self-love, rage, exasperation, and lustfulness urge the slave onward.

I Cannot See You

A highly placed government official came to see a Sufi. In the hope of hearing praise for his actions from the *shaikh* and being favored with his blessing, he said in a self-congratulating manner, "We love and respect the Sufis."

The *shaikh* lowered his head.

"Thanks to you Sufis," continued the visitor, "all ways are open."

The *shaikh* did not seem to have heard him.

"We've done everything so that you should feel safe," said the visitor, now openly praising himself. Then he stopped.

The Sufi was quiet as well. It was as if there was no one else but him in the entire *hanaqa*.

After a while the visitor began to fidget and emitted a polite cough as a reminder of his presence.

Suddenly the *shaikh* roused himself, like a golden eagle, cast a slow glance about the *hanaqa*, and asked that the lights be turned on. The lights came on.

"I cannot see you," said the wise man, looking intently at his visitor.

The visitor glanced around him in surprise and moved closer to the *shaikh*. "I'm here, Your Grace."

The Sufi asked for his glasses, which he hoisted up to his eyes, and then again turned in the direction of his visitor.

"No!" he said sadly. "I cannot see you."

"But I'm right here!" exclaimed the important visitor in bewilderment.

"Your 'I' is sitting in this room," replied the *shaikh* politely. "But you yourself I cannot see."

♦ ♦ ♦

With time the demands of the *nafs* grow disproportion-

ate to the limited abilities of its slave. Then the person's
nafs ammara [132] will often drive him to the path of crime.

And it is written in the Qur'an on this account:

> *The (human) soul is certainly prone to evil.* [133]

◆ ◆ ◆

Behind the unfulfilled desires of the little man lurks an
exulting devil, which humiliates and annihilates the human foundation in its former master. This is why the weak
man is called the slave of his passions. Slaves do not realize
their divine provenance, nor their divine destiny. It is as if
they came from nowhere and are going nowhere. For this
reason they do not fear God, they fear only not carrying
out the will of their *nafs*.

But the Sufi is free as a bird. He depends upon no one,
owes nothing to anyone, and fears only his Lord. And he
is free only because his *nafs* is under his heel and with each
step he grinds it into sand and then into dust. The Sufi is
a man who has grasped the truth of separation, liberation
from self, from his *nafs* and its lowly yearnings.

◆ ◆ ◆

The Sufi Abu Said ibn Abi al-Khair said:

132 *Nafs ammara*: the soul that incites to evil.
133 Qur'an 12:53

Sufism is glory amid stagnation, wealth amid poverty, satiety amid famine, finery amid nakedness, freedom amid slavery, life amid death, and sweetness amid pungency....

The Sufi is one who rejoices in all that the Lord does, so that God should rejoice in all that the Sufi does.

Such a condition—say the *shaikhs*—is attained only when the Sufi ceases to pay attention to his "I," the great source of all suffering, and becomes filled with love and yearning for God. The Sufi is he who displays diligence in the *amr bil' magruf* and the *nakhi an munkar*.[134]

♦ ♦ ♦

The *nafs* does not give in immediately but rather constantly tries to attract attention, to draw the man away from considerations of eternity toward the feelings, desires, and passions of today. But the Sufi is indifferent and pitiless toward the *nafs*. He gives in to it on no account, indulging it in nothing. The man who remembers God does not compete with his *nafs*, he reforms it. His *nafs* changes in accordance with his progress along the path, taking on a new shape and becoming filled with spiritual sense.

The Sufi is humility. Humility presupposes dissolution.

---

134 *Amr bil' magruf*: actions in accord with the injunctions of the *shari'at*. *Nakhi an munkar*: the struggle against all things proscribed by Islam (author's note).

The dissolution of all human desires and caprices in the all consuming love for one's Lord. The Sufi ceases to set himself in opposition to the earthly world. He has no need of competing with anyone for a place in the sun. This world is to him merely a road along which he is walking to God.

◆ ◆ ◆

They say that the incomparable Hazrat Yusuf Hamadani, may mercy be upon him, was a man of astounding politeness. He addressed people in a gentle smile and was soft spoken. He addressed whomever he met as *hodja* and was always the first to extend a greeting.

They say that his fear before God made him cry a great deal. And when he spoke of himself, he never used the word "I," but most often in reference to himself substituted the words "this wretch."

He stood up for every person who entered the *hanaqa* and respected the opinions of others. He spoke little and forbade his *murids* to speak over much. And they say, too, that our teacher looked more often sad than joyful on the outside.

It's Better When They Call Me Crazy

A man came to a Sufi and demanded, "Some people call you crazy, others say you're wise. Who's right?"

"Both," answered the Sufi with a smile, "for wisdom and

insanity are fruits of the same tree. When the fruit is green, I'm crazy. When, with time, it matures, perhaps I'm wise."

"But isn't it better when they call you wise," asked the man more calmly.

"It's better when they call me crazy," answered the Sufi.

"Why?" asked the man in genuine surprise.

"Because most often," said the Sufi, "insanity is a higher form of wisdom, where there is no need to answer stupid questions, only to relate to God."

✦ ✦ ✦

The ordinary man is distinct from the world, he sets himself in opposition to it and wants to take from it what he supposes belongs to him by right. He struggles, overcomes difficulties that he himself has created, striving to leave a trace in this merciless, beautiful, and—to him—alien world. Hence his striving for glory, wealth, and honors.

He grabs everything that might come in handy, drawing it towards him, everything that might raise him in the eyes of others like him, competing with the world. Even knowledge he uses in order to feed his inflexible arrogance. Boastfulness, frustration, caustic sarcasm, mercilessness, and arrogance surround his heart like a great wall, and God is not within it.

✦ ✦ ✦

They say that man is weak. But his weakness lies only in his having subjected himself to the *nafs*. This is why the

life of the unbeliever invariably ends in disappointment.
For a man can never fulfill all his desires. Those that have
been fulfilled don't bring satisfaction. Those that haven't
leave a bitter after-taste in one's heart.

The Whole Difference Between Us

A man came to a Sufi and decided to argue with him.

"They call you a Godly man," he began in a confident
voice, gathering himself for debate, "but I don't see any difference between you and me."

"I don't see any either," answered the Sufi.

"Then can I call myself a Sufi too?" asked the man joy-
fully.

"Of course!" answered the Sufi, "If it should so please
Allah, you can call yourself a saint right this minute."

"But there must be some kind of difference between us?"
asked the stranger, completely taken aback. "I'm rich, for
instance, but you're poor."

"Wealth has no meaning before the eye of the Most
High," answered the Sufi.

"What then?" asked the man, not giving up.

"The whole difference between you and me lies in the
fact," answered the Sufi, "that you think always of life, and
I, of death."

✦ ✦ ✦

Desires are the wind beyond which a man is driven

through his entire life. And, it seems, here now, it is close. Yes—there, he's caught it! But what he has caught is only grief and bitterness with the pungent odor of tears and wormwood. The man's life, it would seem, has been lived through, and all that's left is a gaping emptiness, an icy emptiness and fear before the black figure of approaching death.

But the Sufi is free as a bird. In him there is no arrogance, no malice, no rivalry with the world. He is a world unto himself, in which the sole yearning is for his Beloved. Sincerity, goodness, and humility are his righteous traits. He recalls the words of the Qur'an:

> *And I do call to witness the self-reproaching spirit*
> *(that admonishes one to eschew evil).* [135]

He is a slave not of himself but of God in himself. Is this not why Hafiz has said, "The only free men are slaves!"

✦ ✦ ✦

They say that on one occasion his Holiness Sayyid Amir Kulal, may mercy be upon, while still a bachelor, had arranged with several people to wash their clothing, and the friends set out for one of the gardens in the settlement of Ramitan. When the clothes had be washed, they wanted to dry them, and his Holiness Amir Kulal said:

"Do not spread your clothes on the burrs of the fence lest you harm them, and do not hang them in the trees lest

---

135   Qur'an 75:2.

you break the branches, and do not spread them on the ground lest you spoil the livestock's food."

His surprised friends asked, "But Amir, how will you dry your clothing?"

And Amir said, "I shall spread it on my back and wear it in the sun until it dries."

And then his Holiness Amir said:

"O my friends, if a tiny bit of the fence or a branch of a tree should break, or if the livestock's food should be spoiled, what would you say to the owner of this garden in your defense? Be careful not to consider an impermissible act as being of little consequence, no matter how small it might seem, because from the fact that a man considers a sin insignificant, he goes to hell. Thus did his Holiness the Prophet, peace be his, say: 'There are no little sins when one is obstinate. There are no big ones when one appeals to the Lord.'"

And his Holiness Amir Kulal also said:

"The Most High Lord does not reveal the path to anyone until that person makes piety his life's goal."[136]

✦ ✦ ✦

We have taken in the fundamental positions from the collection of moral rules indicated by Muhammad Sadyki-i-Kashgari, may mercy be upon him. But there are many other treatises in which different rules and injunctions for the beginning Sufi have been compiled. Let us briefly turn to some of these, as discussed by Mukhammad Amin al'-

---

136   *Wisdom of the Sufis*, pp. 45-46 (author's note).

Kurdi al'-Erbili in his *Book of Eternal Gifts*. The *murid* is recommended:

- To maintain ritual purity for as long as possible after performing ablutions
- To employ the time between the first and second evening prayers for the performance of *zikr*
- To avoid, as much as possible, people who censure the Sufis or doubt the truth of the *tariqat's* doctrine or practice. Observance of this injunction guarantees the *murid's* attainment of his end on the path to God, while, by contrast, neglect of this injunction and socializing with those who criticize the "people of the secret," will cause a shroud to fall over the *murid's* heart, which prevents the light of Truth from penetrating within
- To eat, drink, wear clothing, and make use of an abode only according to the allowances of the religion, for he who employs the *haram*[137] will never attain to God's presence until he renounces that which is forbidden
- To display absolute humility. The Sufi sees himself as the last among divine creatures, more lowly than any other, and assumes that he would be worthy of punishment and heavenly retribution were it not for the mercy of Allah
- To turn one's attention to the sins of one's own

---

137 *Haram*: the foods, articles of clothing, and so on, forbidden in Islam (author's note).

soul and not to other people's sins or shortcomings.
If a Sufi should begin to look at the shortcomings
of another person, he should know that that sinful
person is like a mirror that reflects the Sufi's own
sin. [138]

◆ ◆ ◆

They say that the Sufi does not only perfect his disposition in the *hanaqa* or at home, by remembering the name
of God in quiet seclusion. He can do this everywhere and
at every moment. An instant without the remembrance of
God becomes an irretrievably lost moment for the heart's
purification.

But of course the Sufi at an early stage finds his highest school in the *hanaqa*, where the *talib* takes part in the
discussions that the *shaikh* leads with his pupils. Hazrat
Alisher Navoi, may mercy be upon him, said that by taking
part in such discussions "one may attain great successes on
the path even with small efforts." [139]

And Hazrat Navoi also said:

Let each participant compare his time in the discussion with the past. If he discovers a flaw within

138   Shaikh Mukhammad Amin al'-Kurdi al'-Erbili, *The Book of
Eternal Gifts: On the Worthy and Laudable Qualities of the Naqshbandi
Sufi Brotherhood and its Path to God* (Russian). Ufa: 2000, pp. 211-12
(author's note).
139   Alisher Navoi. "Hodja Bahauddin." In *Star of the East* (Russian),
Nos. 11-12, p. 123 (author's note).

himself, then let him consider it his duty to interact with those who have come to know God. [140]

During the discussions with his brothers on the path, the Sufi learns to see his flaws and remove them. A brother will never insult him through an inconsiderate word. Even when he sees the errors that an inexperienced *murid* commits, he will imitate the tact and wisdom of his *shaikh* and never openly comment on them—by necessity this will be an indirect comment, a parable, or a story remembered by chance, in which the protagonist makes the same mistakes.

When he hears such a story, the *talib* understands without fail and never again commits the same errors. And for the brother who so tactfully corrected him quiet gratitude will remain in his heart.

There are many legends and narratives about friendships among the Sufis, a fact to which the following pronouncement by Imam al-Bukhari, may mercy be upon him, testifies:

"Abu Musa heard that the Prophet, may Allah bless and greet him, said:

> Verily, in the relations among them right believers must resemble the separate parts of a structure that strengthen each other mutually, and in so saying,

140   Ibid, p. 123 (author's note).

may Allah bless and greet him, he interlocked the fingers of his hands."[141]

* * *

The path to righteousness is a long and difficult path to divine light, the result of spiritual and physical exertion, the purification and ennoblement of a person's moral nature in accordance with the moral traits and foundations of the Prophet Muhammad, may Allah bless and greet him, for he said:

God has sent me for perfecting the foundations of morality.

Such moral qualities of the person as gentleness, meekness, mercy, self-sacrifice, kindness, friendliness, nobility, altruism, forgiveness, magnanimity, generosity, humility and truthfulness, self-disparagement, the belittling of one's own worthy qualities, the ability to find such qualities in others—these are the traits for which the Sufi battles every day and every God given moment.

* * *

Until my tongue learns not to pronounce the word "I" and my soul becomes as obedient to my self as a little

---

141   Imam al-Bukhari. *Al-Jami as-Sahik.* In *Zvezda Vostoka,* No. 5 (1992), p. 7 (author's note).

puppy following its master, I will not be worthy of God. This saddens me most of all.

✦ ✦ ✦

According to the testimony of Abu Malik al-Harith bin Asim al-Ashari, [142] may mercy be upon him, who said:

"The Messenger of Allah, may Allah bless him and send him peace, said:

"'Purity is half of faith.... Prayer is light, a Godly deed is proof, patience is illumination, and the Qur'an is an argument for or against you. Each person begins his day himself and acts as a vendor of his soul, either liberating it or leading it to destruction.'" [143]

He who wishes to rise up must show humility. He who wishes to become righteous must form the traits of nobility and generosity within him. There is no other path to God.

---

142   Abu Malik Al-Harith bin Asim Al-Ashari: source of *ahadith*.
143   *Hadith* cited by Muslim (author's note).

Index of Names and Terms